Business
by Faith

A Journey of Integrating the Four D's of Success

Still Standing

Linda L. Smith

ZOE LIFE Publications, Inc.

Riverside, CA

Business by Faith © 2015 by Linda L. Smith

Volume III: Still Standing

ISBN 13: 978-1-934556-74-0

Library of Congress Control Number: 2015901716

Published by: **Zoe Life Publications, Inc.**
Post Office Box 310096
Fontana, CA 92331

Editor: Linda L. Smith

Cover Design: Jiong Li and Amanda Johnson

Printed in the United States of America

Table of Contents

Linda L. Smith

Introduction

Oh my, oh my, I'm *Still Standing!*

Integrating the Four D's of Success into my personal and professional journey continues to be one of the most exciting experiences of my entire life as I build and grow an educational institution that imparts both knowledge and inspiration.

Up to this point, my personal journey has been presented for you to glean, critique, experience, and learn from. I have withheld nothing in my attempt to enlighten and encourage you to press in to ALL that God has called you to, and to do so without apology!

Within the pages of Volume III, *Still Standing*, you will realize the value of having sheer determination and its importance to your day-to-day activity. You must be headstrong about pursuing your goals and objectives with an unshakeable confidence that is rooted and grounded in faith and not people. People will come and go as they serve their purpose in your life — you must remain focused and believe by faith that with God, anything is possible regardless of what it looks like.

And equally important, you must add to that faith a knowing that the Lord is well able to see you through whatever your journey in life brings you.

Like me, my friend — you're ***Still Standing***!

With Love,

Linda Lee Smith

Linda L. Smith

Business by Faith

Journal 6

Begins: July 2, 1999 ~ 11:33 p.m.

Ends: March 31, 2000 ~ 11:00 p.m.

7/2/99 ~ 11:33 p.m.

Busy straightening out the liability insurance issue for Sturges Arts for the graduation.

Ernell came through. Rosina with Union Bank informed me that the $750,000 was approved. Now, we wait on the SBA loan for $60,000. Four-D must come up with $50,000. I was too tired to get excited. I called the Department of Ed and spoke with Erick about our status for approval. After a long explanation, I was finally told our application was forwarded for signature to Washington. We will receive a three-year approval. Lord, thank You. The ETP monitor is coming Tuesday. Betty works until 9:00 p.m. preparing.

Tomorrow is the graduation. I am the speaker. Topic – gratitude. What is there to be grateful for? I received a letter from a young lady from Alabama. She graduated from an RN program. She failed the National Council Licensure Examination (NCLEX) test three times. I shared with her, encouraged her, provided advice to take a test, and prayed with her. We will keep in touch. She will schedule to test 9/1/99. God, keep her focused and encouraged. Tired, sleepy, goodnight.

7/12/99 ~ 10:38 a.m.

Happy Anniversary, Ernell and Linda.

God blessed you to reach 24 years of marriage. Well, life has been full of twists, turns, tears, shock, happiness, sadness, joy, pain, and peace. We have survived. We now look forward to life together.

Ernell is my rock. He steadies me when I waver emotionally on unsteady nerves. He is always there when I return from a journey searching for me and happiness. It was always there, with him. He loves me, protects me, feeds me, clothes me, and holds me tenderly with strong arms of love.

My life is good at home. I am happy. We went to Cambria for the weekend. We stayed at San Simon Resort across the street from the Pacific Ocean. What a relaxing, wonderful weekend. We walked miles along the ocean, holding hands, talking, laughing, and taking pictures. We watched the sunset. Oh, what a beautiful sight, the sun slowly sitting upon the horizon, and then quickly disappearing. Bright, shining rays turning into a beautiful orange soft glow and then sinking into blackness. God's wonder.

My swelling totally dissipated. Ankles normal, feet pretty small. I am so grateful to be here. Air fresh, food delicious, exercise. Limited thoughts of the school = stress. I asked Ernell if Cherry could be the V.P. of Four-D Success Academy. He said yes. She knows the school better than anyone. God will guide me.

I love Ernell. I look forward to tomorrow. Lord, thank You. Linda

7/14/99 ~ 11:10 p.m.

We received a 3-year Provisional Approval from the Department of Ed. Its good until 6/30/2002. We must address the ABHES findings by September 30th. We will make the deadline. We received verbal approval from Upland Convalescence Hospital for the Work Study Program. Tomorrow, Carol Wagner DON will sign the agreement.

Rubidoux Community Hospital is receiving the concept. Deanna Price Adm. feels the owner will buy into the program. I submitted a letter to Thomas Shu requesting a decrease in the sale price to

$126,000. And he fixed the code items. He came back with $20,000 reduction.

I had a telephone meeting with Greg Sheets and Mike Ballard. We realize that the price must come down in order for Four-D to successfully manage the building. Friday the 16th is the final day. Either it is Four-D's or not. I will start looking immediately.

As I thought about the steps of acquisition and cost, I realized I have learned so much.

Assessment of the building – City Planner, Architect drawings, bids from contractions, contract review, cost acquired, meeting with Economic Development Agency. Financial reports to SB County Economic Development Department. Financials to Books, Cost/Development, assessment cost, environmental reports, elevator report from DSHA, air quality management report for hazardous materials. State Department of Child Care contracts, applications for direct loans, guarantee loans. Due diligence period, service debt, negotiations, and more.

All of it is a learning experience for me.

Cherry and I spoke briefly about our stressed relationship and her position/role with the school. She is preparing to depart. I am at peace. I must stay focused and press forward.

Lord, thank You for peace, Linda.

7/15/99 ~ 1:44 PM

The beginning of a new diary. Actually, I had filed the previous one last month. I have been making entries on notepaper. That process leaves too many loose papers, so here I am.

So many thoughts and emotions are not reflected in my writings. I have come to experience love, joy, sadness, disappointment, peace, discontentment, anxiety, awareness, truth, honesty, deceit, failure, and success. I have hundreds of experiences that could fill a hundred books.

I thought about writing a novel. I have much to share. As I think about my life, the path I have traveled, I imagine the possibilities of being a successful author.

I have much to give; I am intelligent, knowledgeable about business, and how to start and keep it alive. I am innovative, daring. I seek opportunities to share FDSA.

Many people have come and gone in my work life. I feel that I am at a crossroad with Cherry. Although I am not clear on many issues with her, I feel she is angry and disillusioned regarding our relationship. I think the Essence article on "How I Did It" made her feel left out. I had no idea of the language of the Essence article or title until I read it. She has expressed that she has no interest in expanding the school. She is sick of the nursing program. She has started her own company. When the dust settles, I will be standing. It is so unfortunate that outside influences and negative comments can have such a strong impact on a friendship. I have journeyed down many paths. People of yesterday are faint memories in my mind.

Today, I visited Sun Rise Palomares and Ember Care Convalescent Hospitals seeking contracts to train CNA. Met with Virginia Garcia, who I worked with in 1992, at Ember. Highly possible I will receive a contract to train at Ember or even with the Corporation. I will pick up the Upland Com. Hospital contract today.

Tomorrow, I meet with Thomas, Mike, and Greg about the building. If it is ours, fine – or God will direct my steps.

Lord, at times, it feels like too much to handle. I receive comfort in knowing You. Aisha called this week. She has found her purpose in life. She will always have something to do for the Lord. My child.

3:16 p.m.

Not only did I obtain the agreement with Upland, Carol Wagnes and I discussed state supported training for the LVN programs and CEN Training for the hospital. Looking positive. Off to Colton.

7/16/99 ~ 10:45 a.m.

Well, the deal did not go through. The seller was not willing to lower the price to meet our needs. I returned the keys and environmental report, shook hands, and called Rosina and left a message. Greg came by and helped. We knew going in that I had to accept financial limits and stay within theirs ($1.5 million tops). Mike is positive we will start to look again. I know we are going to land on our feet. Financially, things look bright. We will receive the $20,000 back to our account.

Lord, guide us.

Well, now I must attend the Women of Distinction Luncheon. I am a judge. Have a blessed day, all.

7/20/99

I feel great. No sorrow over the building. Forge ahead to something better and bigger. We are recruiting for the Work Study Program. Fourteen students for Hampton Broswell to start Monday, the 26th. I met with Virginia Garcia and her husband, Conrad. They are installing vending machines at Four-D Success Academy. I struck up a conversation about foreign students exchange programs. INS application. Conrad's sister works for the INS. He will obtain information regarding sponsorship and the requirement to have foreign clients for training. I want to do international training. This may be the door.

Tomorrow, I have an appointment with VP Ember Care April Abrerage to discuss training for the Work Study Program and CNA Training. Peace is in the house. Changed intake process to capture more students. Low enrollment in the Pharmacy and Med billing class, but I know that is going to change.

Lord, thank You for PEACE.

7/21/99 ~ 7:24 a.m.

Where will the Lord have me to go? I am looking for another building, possibly Rialto. I will travel to New Orleans in August. I am preparing to review a Psychiatric Tech program and the Surgical Tech Program. I will attend the Pilipino Expo on Saturday. I seek information exchange. God is guiding my path. Margie and I spoke about the exchange or sponsorship program. Margie's husband was reading the paper on the 20th, and low and behold, the article he was reading was the upcoming expo. Today, Mr. Garcia will provide info on sponsorship.

I will be back. Time to go to work.

7/21/99 ~ 11:11 p.m.

I had a good meeting with April – V.P. Operation of Pleasant Care. I explained the program. We had dialogue. She received the course of training to present to the president. She indicated it was a good program and they needed help. She asked if I would consider a cooperate contract to train in California. Yes, 12-15 hospitals. I informed her I was also very interested in a contract to provide Continued Education. She was pleased to hear this information. A discussion to come. I reacquainted myself with Cora – a nurse from Driftwood Conv Hosp. We never know who will cross our path. Following this meeting, I made a call to Pomona Valley Medical Center. Although I did not see the Director of Education, I did see Tahira. We discussed contacts in the hospital. She introduced me to her boss. I left. Off to see Tommy Morrow of Inland Valley News Paper. He provided support and advice on marketing the Academy. He emphasized I am Four-D Success, Press release to papers monthly (weekly), and use the Essence article to promote the school. He shared his concern of jealousy in the camp. Cherry could not follow my directions. His insight moved me. I departed and headed for Rialto. Cold call on the Redevelopment Director, Bob Barlett. We discussed options for the Academy in receiving waivers or deferment on fees and permits. He was open and positive. I then went to see Barbara McGee, City Clerk. Discussed the 'Ross Vacancy' she called Cyrous — the owner. We spoke. He will consider lease to purchase. Back at the office, Mike and I speak. An appointment is set up for tomorrow at 9:00 a.m. to see the building. Stephen and I discuss issues of development and roles of person. Availability and accountability. If he is putting limitations on who can call him, then I will not pull him into the development circle. I can't depend on him. After clarification, clearly stating my goals and firm commitment to Four-D, he understood. I will not jeopardize the school over anyone. I was going to move forward.

He was pleased to hear my statements. He was concerned if I would let friendship control my decision-making. We discussed New

Orleans, Washington, Arizona, Atlanta, and Texas, expansion in California and program development of the Surgical Tech and Psychiatric Tech Program. All of it can happen.

Lord, keep me focused. Guide my path. Let me always be true to the Academy, its purpose, and people.

7/22/99 ~ 11:26

Today, I looked at another building. 1521 Riverside Dr, Rialto. High rent, don't know if it will fly.

Appointment tomorrow with Deanna Price. Rubidoux about contracts. This evening, Donna Bostic gave me a sculpture by Thomas Black Shears called 'The Comforter.' A tall erect female embracing a child, intricate detail of hand, face, feet, and eyes. It brought me to tears. I shared the name Umuhoza, The Comforter. The Lord will lead my path. Today, Sandra Richardson called my office, asked me to speak at the Executive Business Women's Conference in Laughlin, Nevada, on October 2nd. They will pay for hotel, flight, etc. I am so excited. Tommy Morrow's words of yesterday came true today.

The future is bright.

Thanks, Lord.

I am going to New Orleans, LA, on August 12th-15th to meet with Mona Houston.

7/24/99 ~ 12:00

On Friday, I received a call from Sam Dunkin, an employee of Pleasant Care. Called to inquire if I would be interested in selling Four-D Success Academy, Inc. I was pleasant, I laughed, and I was honored. But it's not for sale. We had a laugh. I said, "Sam, if I were

15

to sell, what would you offer?" His response was, "I never bought a school before." I laughed and said, "I never sold a school before." He asked if he could call me back next week. Why not?

Greg and Charlie said a product could start another business. I told Charlie Four-D is my child. I would not sell my child. He amused me. Find out what the child is worth.

Ernell was informed. He thought for a while and made his face. Are you going to sell – no. Only I know the covenant I have with God. The success of the school is not measured in dollars. The success of the school is measured in the number of lives it has touched. There is no money that can touch so many as Four-D Success. It is the foundation. Through God, all things are possible.

Goodnight, Lord.

7/25/99 ~ 11:04

A good day. Awakened by the gentle touch of my husband. It is so good to be in love. My soul is satisfied. I lay still quietly, thoughts of him, our life.

We spend the day together. At home early, hanging around the house, me on the computer, sending e-mails, reading. He is working on the truck. We went to Mama Julie's, picked up meds. Visited sites I had looked at. I asked for his opinion. WHERE DO I GO? We discussed locations, and then were off to Mama Vivian's for a quick spell, home after stopping by the Dairy Queen for ice cream. At home, I read and sorted mail. He fired up the grill, dinner, and conversation. We laugh lightly. Life is good. Sitting under the dimness of a light, I squint to read. Ernell walks over and turns the light up. He asked, "Isn't that better?" I thank him and remind him of his role to take care of me. He does.

I prayed today for much, I give thanks for all. God hears and answers. I must believe – have faith.

Tomorrow is a new day. Lord, thank You. Your Child, Linda

$7/28/99 \sim 6:22$ a.m.

Yesterday, I viewed another building. I know it is not in my heart. On the night of 7/27, I dreamed I was standing in front of the building on Valley crying. Mike was by my side. I was sorry for him. He has spent many hours with me seeking a new home for the school. This industrial site with three separate buildings does not allow me to create the image and flow I seek. I am saddened. I know God is looking. He will guide me. I was introduced to Nick Gonzales, Assistant to Nick Mayor Valles Office, by Leah Cash. I shared my desires with him. He will keep his eyes open. I feel such negativity and tension with Cherry. I had to speak with her regarding the program hours/calculations for financial disbursements. She blew up saying she was about "sick of this shit and has had it up to here." Stress is anxiety created inward. I have allowed anxiety to overcome me, tingling in my left upper and lower extremities. I lie still at 3:00 a.m. listening to my heartbeat. I pray. I toss and turn, and I pray for solutions.

I asked Cherry for her resignation. The environment is very unhealthy. Lord, guide us all to peace.

$8/1/99 \sim 11:40$ a.m.

Numbers 32:1-12

Don't settle for 2nd best. Children coming out of Israel had seen a land suitable for cattle. They ask to settle in that land rather than going to the land of Jordan, that which God had promised them.

I came to Church today for a personal blessing. I need to feel the spirit of understanding. My heart is heavy with the negativity in the school. My heart is burdened with finding a new site. I was considering settling for something that was 2nd best. I know I can't take that building. God has a better place for us. I know He will clean the house. Place us where we need to be. I pray for Cherry. I feel she is dividing the camp. She is unhappy with me – not the school. But I am the school, the senior representative. God blessed me. He guided me. He will do all that is necessary for us, the school. Lord, thank You for bringing me here today. I opened up the well and the tears flowed. The words came, the prayers went up, and the blessings came down. Lord, thank You.

8/1/91 ~ 4:47 p.m.

My letter to God.

Dear Lord,

Today I awaken, tossing thoughts in my mind. I need to go to Church. There is a message for me. You know my thoughts and my burdens. I rise to hear Your Word.

No one will ever know what You said to me on July 31, 1991 at 1:05 a.m. I have been given a task so great. Lord, I cry, seeking understanding. Am I lost? That can't be for I am with You!

I have grown so much. I asked You for wisdom. When I receive it, I must use it. Have I not been wise in my actions? Have I let too much water pass under the bridge. I must maintain control. You have sent Your message through so many messengers. I listen, but not act. I can't lead others if I do not follow You! I dedicate my life to You and Four-D Success Academy. I will act as a messenger to protect, to grow. You have given me such responsibilities. Today at Church, a member, Pat, thanked me for what I do. "We need to help our black people. We need to help everyone. Linda, I am proud of you." Her words ring in my ears.

I don't truly know the effect I have on others through the school. I guess I am special; I have done something special through You.

In the pit of my soul, I cry, unable to express to others what the school means to me. You have blessed me so. When I was asked to sell, I laughed. How can I sell God's property! Lord, as I seek a new home, I see time running out. In 10 months, my lease will expire 6/2000. Lord, where will you have us go? Today, the message spoke words to my heart. Tears of understanding moved me, "Don't settle for less." The thoughts I had of the industrial buildings in their individual sections. I was settling for less. I cry, not knowing. But I must stop. Lord, I know You will open new doors. I say, "I can't afford $27,000 a month for rent." Then I stop. I recall the $700 for rent at the first site. We moved in the current space paying $5,200 a month. We currently pay $10,000 a month. Surely, God can provide the additional $17,000. My Lord, I know You have endless funds.

I weep today with a full heart. I left Your house with a new look and hope! Faith stronger.

I must go to the passage of time, pain, hope, and false fears to get the benefit of You. How I wasted time in fear, worry, and sadness when You promised joy and the fulfillment of my requests.

Have I not asked, being too busy to cry and worry? All I need to do is ask. Lord, I ask for a prayer house, a prayerful school.

Lord, I asked that You give peace and comfort.

Lord I ask that the thorns be removed. The thorns of jealousy and envy.

Lord, I ask for new walls to house Four-D Success Academy.

Lord, I ask for the financial blessing to help others.

Lord, I ask for wisdom to do the right thing.

Lord, I ask for support to expand the school's philosophy. Through God, all things are possible.

Lord, thank You for this day, my life, my home, my family.

Thank You. Your Child, Linda

Happy Birthday to Me!

8/7/99

Today, I am forty-seven years old. 1952 was a long time ago, yet a blink in the eyes of the Lord. I am still His Child.

Today, Ernell and I are going to San Diego Old Town to spend some loving time together. Last evening, he, Earl, mom, and I saw B.B. King live. At the age of 73, he can still bring the house down with his sweet, mellow blues. The staff presented me with a watch yesterday. I laughed saying they still liked me. My old watch was faded and thoughts had entered my mind to purchase another one. Well, that's done. I received a call from Virginia Garcia with Ember Care. They are ready to start the training program with us. Monday, we will sign the contract.

We are excited about the work-study program. We are recruiting for the Vocational Nurse Program. The goal is 45 students. We will continue to pursue the course. We are working on all of the programs.

I had a talk with Cherry. She wrote a letter of apology for the rudeness and disrespect to me. I accepted. We discussed the school briefly, her relationship with Stephen, and the role with the partnership she was forming. I indicated I needed top managers to communicate. I can't move forward if they could not relate business issues. I also told Cherry she could not serve two masters: Four-D and her partnership. I need 110% of her to address the company needs. She understood. Sadiq called and sang Happy Birthday to me. It was a sweet sound!

Well, I must get up. My husband is washing clothes, mopping the floor, and he has vacuumed the floors. Life is good!

Lord, thank You for another day.

P.S. I saw the inside of the 1020 Washington building – 30,000 sq ft. Good possibilities. I'll see what God will do.

8/11/99 ~ 7:02 a.m.

Ernell and I had a wonderful time on Saturday and Sunday. We arrived in San Diego on Saturday afternoon. No reservations for a room. We were fortunate. We ended up at the West Gate Hotel for only $140.00, an elegant 4 star hotel. Lovely room with room service. The evening was great; we walked, holding hands and talking. We had a great tasty dinner at the Coyote. I had tequila lime shrimp! Over ate, but goooood!

Sunday, we walked the pier, had lunch/brunch, then headed home. What a wonderful Birthday turning 47.

Cherry and I talked about Four-D Success, its future, and her desires and frustrations. We will work through it all. I am sure of myself as President/CEO. I told her I am a better leader today than I was a year

21

ago. I desire that she stay only because I truly believe she was God-sent – otherwise I have no problem with her departure. I know God will guide and protect the Academy. She will progress towards V.P. level. But control, yes. I am in control and it must be maintained. The focus of the school cannot get lost.

Lord, thank You.

8/12/99 ~ 6:55 a.m.

Yesterday, I visited the old Four-D Success Academy training site. I had gone to B of A to obtain cash for my trip to New Orleans. Looking over the brick wall, I found myself staring at the letters and the lamp in the window. I decided to take a closer look. As I ascended the stairs, I recalled the many trips up and down them. I saw the faces of Adenia and Shirley, I could feel the joy of the old days. As I approached the tip of the stairs, I stared at the flooring. The rocks in the cement, new railing painted brown. The windows were dirty but visibility was good. As I looked through the windows, I smiled as I recalled the classes I taught, the furniture there, a desk here, the door open to the storage room, shelves empty as we had left them. I recalled putting them up. I smiled. I looked through the window where my office was. I saw the desk and orange chairs, the telephone outlet. I stepped back from the window and studied each letter in the words of the school's name. I examined the lamp. I recited its words. I thought of Dawn Grimes. She did a good job. All is here as she had placed it. I leaned forward and touched the window. I felt a burst of energy. I radiated inside and I prayed. I went back to the past to understand the present, to pray for the future. I traveled back to August 2, 1992 when I moved into the office. I thanked God. He has brought the school and me far. I prayed to God for wisdom and peace. I thanked Him for the first home. I thanked Him for the new home to come. I asked for the best site, I asked that He make a way out of no way. I askd that He touch the ears of those needing a touch. He knows my heart, my prayer, and my needs. I thankd Him for my family. He has blessed me. I feel whole. I descend the stairs. I sit in my car and I feel God's presence. He tells me everything is all right. I believe, I receive. I rejoice in the spirit. I smile. He does speak to me.

Lord, thank You.

On Delta Airlines, I travelled to New Orleans, LA, to assess a potential site to expand. Steven traveled to Washington D.C. last week. He and Cherry had a two-hour meeting on Friday. I will meet with them Monday. What is in store? I will enjoy New Orleans. I fly on the wings of God. I am safe.

His child, Linda. Kenner, New Orleans

8/12/99 ~ 11:15 p.m.

I arrived safely in New Orleans as expected. I fly on the wings of the Lord. Safety assured. I took a cab to Mona Houston Apt. The ride was pleasant. The Cabbie, Sam, and I talked and laughed all the way. He joked about his day, his wife, the hot weather, San Francisco.

I arrived not to hot weather, but I could feel the moisture in the air humidity about 70%. Up the stairs to #206. *Knock, knock, ring the doorbell.* Finally, the door opened. To my surprise, Mona was home. Her plans had changed. She had waited for me. I was greeted with open arms, a hug, and a big smile. What a welcome. We talked and laughed. She was happy I was a guest in her home and I was thrilled to be the guest. She and her daughter, 16-year-old Simona, meshed well. Mona called her mother to tell her I was here. How nice to be special. I took it all in stride. The Essence article. I am here to research opportunities for expansion.

We had dinner with Roy, Mona's friend, at the Jargar Restaurant. We had blackened fish, crab, lobster, crawfish, gumbo, creamy spud potatoes, and garlic bread. Not bad. I was taken to West or East Jefferson Medical Center, a huge 550-bed facility with 750 physicians on the roster. The lobby looked like a fine hotel!

I got excited, juices flowing, mind thinking of all the possibilities. Off to the French Quarters to walk around. Not too crowded, jazz, alcohol, happy people. I stopped by the Pearl Shop, smiled, and moved on. We returned home. Slightly tired, I checked out the newspaper and telephone book for info. Tomorrow, I will call to make contact. Goodnight.

Thanks for a good day.

8/14/99

Yesterday was a day - out by 7:15 a.m. with Mona. Time for business! Tim's office. He and Mona received the presentation she had put together for a physician. We will work together, establishing a physician management network. She is good. Off to the Physician's office they went. I went to hospitals close by. Bencor Hospital. Spoke with Mary, the receptionist. No one around – it is not 9:00 a.m. yet. She told me to come back in 30 minutes. I walked across the street to Turo Infirmary. Waited 10 minutes and met with Lynn Jones, Professional Recruiter. We discussed the need for "professional" staff. She noted a shortage in nurses and other professionals, a lack of professionalism by employees, and a lack of quality in the welcoming of students. Turo is a teaching facility. I will call Lynn next week for follow-up. I want information on salary scales.

I deported and walked to a Pharmacy. The Pharmacist was of no help, but the tech was. She informed me the state was changing the ratio from 1:1 to 1:2 for Pharmacist and Tech.

I got a box of matches for Wendy. Back to Bencor Hospital, had not seen the person for me to speak with. So I waited. I shared a business card with her and why I was in town. Asked if a number I had was local. She allowed me to use the telephone. Made calls to PPC's, Nursing Board, Department of Commerce, Department of Labor, Women's Services Government Office, and multiple calls to speak with various individuals.

The Nursing Board has a hold on new programs. The curriculum requires 600 hours of Med Search. Hospitals are not able to accommodate the students due to the low census on the Med floor. Students are staying in the program longer than planned. The hold has been since 1994. There are 30 applicants waiting to start a VN Program. Spoke with Orleans and Jefferson P/C. Unsure of new changes for 2000. Placed on mailing list for Orleans. I will call Mike Garvey with the Jefferson in for Proposal info.

Met with Mark Jeffs, Director Of Nurses of Bencor Skilled.

- Need qualified staff.
- Need professional staff.
- Need people who will come to work.
- Hire 10 CNA – 1 will stay.
- Highly questioned training skills.
- He welcomes FDSA – no problem with facility agreement. 190-bed facility with 170 patients.

- Received the number to Corp office, I would like to discuss training for Continued Education Units to corp. level/wide. Bencor has 60 Hospital.
- 1 in Claremont.

Toured area with Mona. Visited East Jefferson, an awesome Hospital with a mall lobby. Beautiful. Spoke with receptionist in Personnel. Obtained names and numbers of persons to call by next week. Great lunch; fried chicken breast, peas, and macaroni! Lord, Mona and I brainstormed.

I got a good feel of her knowledge base and work ethics. How can I work with her?

We discussed which programs would work, what the doctors need with medical billers, managers, new curriculum. But location, this stuff is exciting.

We had positive energy. We arrived back home at 4:35 p.m. a full day! Rested, talked, and collaborated more. Waited for Roy before heading off to Biloxi, Mississippi Casino for dinner. Lord, the food is great. Worth the hour and fifteen minute drive, and the twenty minute wait. Ate too much, but so what.

I have been treated well by Mona, Somona, and Roy. We have laughed and worked. Lord, this is good. I know it. Guide our path. You know my heart desires to help. You will make a way. Thank You for introducing me to Mona Houston. The sister from San Diego who works in New Orleans!

Today, Somona and I will go to the Soul Circus while Mona goes to work.

Later

8/15/99 ~ 5:38 a.m.

Well, we did not make it to the Circus. Yesterday, we started out late, took time to relax and talk. Left at 2:00 p.m. Looked at the layout of the city, called a realtor office, left a message. Good location is on Veterans Blvd and Causeway, a very active main street.

Mona is thinking. Went by Eastern College, will call for brochure. Off to the mall to go shopping. Mona hit it big, me a few pieces, nothing to get excited about. Good dinner at Copeland – my treat. This has been a wonderful trip. New friend, new business venture. We returned home at 10:00 p.m. tired. Well it is now 6:45 a.m. I am at the Airport. My flight leaves (Delta) at 7:35. I sit here thinking of so many things. Returning home to Ernell, telling my mother a lady referred to me as "grandmother." The School, Cherry's possible departure, new school in New Orleans, Washington. Knowing God will provide and protect. I feel peace and calmness. I wonder how Mike Ballard is doing with inquiry on 1020 Washington?

Heavenly Father, I thank You for this wonderful experience, the possibilities You have put before me are energizing. I come to You for guidance and blessings. I appreciate what You have given me. I will do my best to proceed. Thank You, Lord.

8/16/99 ~ 7:15 a.m.

Thoughts in my mind of Cherry abusing the finances of the school, using the credit card to pay for meals, gas, supplies to start CLS, her company. Leaving early to do work not pertaining to the Academy. I will inform her of my concerns today.

8/19/99 ~ 10:28 p.m.

Yesterday, Cherry stated, "I can't stand to look at you. I need to pray or something." At least that is what I heard. Those words plagued me. I was appalled. Silent, I rose for work, arriving at 6:20 a.m. I prayed. I had Wendy call the entire faculty for a meeting at 1:30. I wrote out a subordination letter to Cherry and requested her resignation.

When I called for her at 1:15, I was told she had left the office 5 minutes prior to catch a plane. I pray for her.

She returned the call. I informed her I wanted to discuss her comments of yesterday. She stated she was repeating what Nancy had said, making reference to my comments of apology 3 months ago.

At the staff meeting, I informed the faculty I respected them as professionals and as instructors. I called the meeting to express Linda. I did not feel I was being represented properly. I felt the negative spirit and I had to excise the wound.

As I expressed myself, I watched the attention of the faculty. I emphasized attendance and the importance of faculty professional presentation, my meeting with class 9, their concerns, and my responsibilities. Open discussion — faculty expressed their views and concerns of Administration's response to their needs.

Nancy's comments were challenging and required direct, focused responses. I had to let her know that I was in charge. Nancy resigned at the meeting. She left at the end of the day with her check. I had to ask for her letter of resignation. She wanted to bring an official type form to me on Monday. As the meeting continued, she commented on the faculty being short, the schedule inadequate. I took charge, asked others where the gaps were, what was needed. They volunteered.

Fill the spots. Jeanette and Tony had the schedule fixed in 2 minutes. We prayed, led by Cathleen. I was assured everything would be okay.

I have a better assessment of the program. I informed Cherry I had placed a freeze on the A DON Position. She, Matthew, and Laura would have to run the program. She must be present 8-5 Monday-Friday. I will require total compliance. Four-D will not suffer due to anyone's neglect.

I am at peace this evening. I visited my mother for a while. I dropped off clothes for Donnie's baby.

Ernell and I are leaving at 3:00 a.m. to go camping. I long for the view and the fresh air.

8/23/99 ~ 5:28 a.m.

I had a good time camping at Lake San Antonio, California. Ernell, Michelle Ballard, and I left the house at 3:15 a.m. off to meet the Petes at Glendora off ramp. We arrived at the campsite at – 10:30 a.m. Michelle and Pam, Manual, their mom, kids, and friends were there. We all located around several campsites and settled in for the weekend.

Plenty of food: burgers, links, hot dogs, corn on the cob, burritos, snacks, Mr. Manuals' greens, potato salad, mac and cheese, and brisket. We laughed, but his greens were good.

I skied for the first time in 3-4 years. It felt good to jump into the lake and warm up. I put on my skis and hit it. I was up and going, relaxed, the water flicking in my face. I went outside the wake. I didn't fall. Lower back muscles tightened, and I go a little further, then release. I was done. But I did it. Ernell said it was good to see me get up again.

Back home, Aisha called. She needed $500 to make final payment at 9:00 a.m. By 5:00 p.m., she was calling back crying. She has been blessed with over $500 in anonymous donors. She cried and thanked the Lord.

I tossed and turned. I need to review the American Express bill and telephone bill. My spirit is warning of serious abuse. I could not sleep. Charges for supplies, gas, food, meals for long distance calls, high telephone bill. I see a charge for $54 for paper. Where did it go? I will review and act accordingly.

Well, I have a 6:00 hair appointment. I am off.

Lord, thank You for the messages and Aisha's blessing.

8/24/99 ~ 5:51 a.m.

Yesterday, I shall call the "take charge" day. In light of the V.N. Program operations and financial loss, I stepped up to the helm and issued Administrative directions.

I issued memos to Cherry regarding:

1) No new hire of A DON – freeze on position.
2) Charge cards discontinued AE & Visa's.
3) Cost control.
4) Matthew given directions on responsibilities – NCLE reports, pictures, ordering books, schedule of faculty, asset with interviews of clients.
5) No work, no pay. Faculty working 32 hours getting paid for 40...stopped.
6) Memo regarding faculty not compliance required test for students.
7) Lack of structured orientation for new facility.

I seek positive outcomes. The program has lost thousands of dollars. I must be more responsible to my adm. duties to all faculty, staff, and students.

Four-D Success will continue. I had Mike to offer $1.5 million for the new building. Lord, I will not settle for less than You promised.

Your Child, Linda

8/26/99 ~11:55 p.m.

Oh what a blessed day. I arrived at the Marriot Palm Desert on Wednesday at 7:00 p.m. I was scheduled to be in a room with 3 other women. I desired a room alone. Well, when I checked in, they had not. There were no available rooms. I requested two roll away beds for comfort.

The beds never came and neither did the 3 roommates. God has allowed me to sit still and pray, relax, and seek peace.

I am working the tapes ministry. I am up at 7:00 a.m. and working until 10:30 p.m. I attended 2 seminars, *Rejoicing in Tribulation and Pressing on*. God spoke to my heart by way of the messages. I rejoice in my tribulation. He chose me because I can do it. Adversaries will rise, I will press on. No fear, I press on. Stay focused in the midst of tribulations, press on. I listened intensely, the words ringing in my head. Chosen, press on.

I came to my room. Alone – I kneeled and prayed, prayed, prayed and cried. I thanked the Lord for selecting me. He knows I can. I can. I thank Him for the school, the spirit within. The prayers going up, the blessings coming down. The excising of the wound, my marriage, my husband, Aisha, Tahira, Momma Vivian.

I cry over Aisha's love for God. Use her Lord, let her be a tool to witness to others. I am overjoyed with prayer, joy, shouts of praise to Him. My child, my husband, my child, Tahira, Four-D.

I cry with joy, full of praises. I pray for a new home for the school. I thank God for the gift to come.

I call Ernell and share the blessings, the prayer. He tells me the counter offer came back at $1.6 million. I will call Mike in the morning. I am praying for $1.5. God is good, all the time. He will provide the money. I will not need to use my home money. He keeps us on a spiritual track.

Lord, thank You.

Love Your Child, Linda

8/27/99 ~ 4:15 p.m.

I called Mike this a.m. at 7:30. We discussed the offer. Counter with $1.5 million and include the relocation of 1 tenant. I believe the messages have been so clear. Ask, believe, trust, and receive. As I go through the day serving others, I think only of the next customers. Greetings with a smile, so many women. About 3,000 strong and 600 young women. We are being blessed in Jesus Christ's name.

I have peace and confidence in my life, the school, and my home. Jesus guides me daily. Resting in my room. Lord, thank You for the solitude.

8/29/99 ~ 12:18 a.m.

The last day of the Conference was my blessing. I released the tears of joy, shouts of hallelujah. Praise Jesus name. The speakers were awesome. God's purpose in my life: my calling, letting go of things and people who want to interfere in my blessing. Why did He choose me? But He knows my heart. I listened, I accepted, I rejoiced. God touched the house. He touched the young women. They blessed me with their testimonies. I shared with Charlene Singleton, the President of GWC God's blessing of $2 million approved for a loan. I planted a seed of $10,000 at last years' GWC. As I shared His blessings, I quickly shared Umuhoza, Rwanda, Sadiq's poem, Donna's gift. I asked God what was I to do. I was to donate $10,000 to The Young Women's Conference. There is no reason why young women in need are left out. God will grant the funds to accomplish this mission! $2,000 a month for 5 months or $1,000 a month for ten months! It will be done for it is God's will.

The school is there and so are the funds needed to close the deal. I personally do not have $150,000 or $200,000 for the $2 million loan. But, God does. My banker has an endless supply of funds.

Aisha is home from Ocean City, New Jersey. She worked the summer with Campus Crusade for Christ. She was truly blessed. God moved in a powerful way in her life. She has committed to start a Chapter to recruit African Americans for Christ. She has dedicated her life to work in some way for the Lord.

She started at home with her father and I, sharing the principle love of Christ, His love, her desire to see us in heaven as a family, explained her relationship with Christ with her father.

I am a Mother filled with joy and pride. I am so proud to be Aisha's mother as a witness to her growth and expression for the love of Jesus Christ/God.

Thank you, Lord.

Linda L. Smith

8/30/99 ~ 11:02 p.m.

My spirit was at peace and calmness floated about me. Change is good. I had them holding on, not accepting the words coming out of Cherry's mouth. (That prayer stuff.) Telling me I couldn't go around praying with Federal dollars. I was in shock. Where did she come from? Who had she spoken to? (Prayer stuff.) Want to terminate Kay. Changed her mind. Said Nancy was not a strong Asst. But then she needed her. What did she do? No management decisions. She did not want to reprimand faculty. Asked me, "What do you want me to do?" Cherry missed two deadlines for class starts. Had to write a letter to President of the Vocational Nurse Board for special approval for the April Class. Students dropping. Large loss of dollars.

Cherry submitted a letter, intent to resign in November. 3 months. I am seeking a replacement ASAP. I called Thelma Bledsoe to inquire if she would consider a temporary position. She will think about it, speak with her husband. She will assist with recruitment.

The office was peaceful. Everyone went about their tasks. Salary/payroll made. God blesses us.

Cherry is asking for severance pay. I called Greg for advice. This situation will come to an end very soon.

I will obtain two more facilities for the ETP Program. And I am seeking corporate contracts for Cont. Ed with Pleasant Care Corporation and Upland Convalescence Hospital. Lord, bless these ventures.

9/1/99 ~ 10:50 p.m.

Peace – be still.

Cherry's Departure.

Turmoil within my soul. Changes I don't understand. I heard of my Essence picture being shredded by Nancy. Faculty present. Cherry aware, no comment. The tone of frustration and anger rises from her bowels. I don't understand. What have I done? I apologize for what harm I could have brought to her. I am sorrowful in not knowing how to aid the negative spirit that has invaded the walls of Four-D Success Academy. When did it start? I remember when class 7 or 8 came on board, Cherry's comment on prayer stuff, can't get Federal Dollars and be praying to students. Astonished, I gasped, looking strangely at others. My look caused her to change her words. More softer clarification. The February 1999 class picture. I was excluded from the group. My picture was sent too late. I guess I was given the explanation after I viewed the final product. I never asked why my picture was withheld. She walked out of a meeting in Colorado. No announcement. Went to her room, packed, and changed her flight. Stood over me, in the dining room, and announced, "I am leaving." No comment. A subordinate leaves an in-service meeting. Repercussions to come. Missed the April deadlines for submission of the July class. Had to write a letter of apology and beg to be placed on the Board agenda. August... full of anger, submitted a letter of apology for disrespect of President/CEO.

She withdrew in past months, not understanding the Essence article. She was angry and embarrassed that she was not featured.

She blurted the announcement of, "I started my own business. I have partners, a business registered as Curriculum Learning Systems

(CLS) to develop programs, technology." She wanted VP position but no responsibilities with managers. I say, "You can't serve two masters." She received poor advice. She was misguided; they didn't know how close to the edge I was. I was underestimated. Her many comments of leaving, my reinforcement of God's presence, she should remain with the Academy. She thought I couldn't make it without her? She thought I would wait for her to resign in November? She was shocked with my decision to terminate the business relationship. *Today is my last day? You're asking me to leave this morning?* I responded yes! Final check issued for $6,000. Matthew and Catherine packed her office up.

I removed the school seal, disks, faculty books, and information that needed to be followed up with to the safety of my car. I left a note. If you come in, please leave the keys, pager, and company telephone. Driving home, I cried. *What happened?*

I interviewed three RN's. Interested in hiring two for clinical positions. Spoke with Jean Stevenson RN Director of Nurses for possible position. She will come by Friday. Lord, guide us.

Tahira called. Pomona Valley Community Hospital placed her on Adm. leave with pay. She signed an employee in 5X's at the person's request. They have a clock system and write in system. I spoke with the Director of Human Resource. Mr. John Bones expressed Tahira's character and integrity. I asked for his deepest consideration. He listened.

I called her back. She is concerned about losing her house. I explained God's will, grace, and protection. It is always done. He has a plan.

Lord, thank You.

I thank You, Lord.

I kneel to pray. All I can say is Thank You, Lord. Thank You, Lord. Thank You for peace. Thank You for the support of the staff. Thank You for my family. Thank You for the support of the Advisors Ms. Bledsoe and Charlie. Thank You so much. Thank You for the building, the future, meeting Mona Houston. Lord, thank You.

Thank You for the God's Women's Conference. The messages, the messenger. Thank You for the donation to give $10,000 to the Young Women's Conference.

I am so grateful for the joy and peace in my heart. Thank You for my health. Today, I had Mike accept the $1.6 million dollar offer on the 1020 Washington, Colton. The future home of Four-D Success Academy.

I thank You, Lord.

Today, Charlie received the property in San Bernardino by the Whitney Young Clinic, the future home of the Golf youth site. There is nothing that can separate us from God.

9/5/99 ~ 8:06 a.m.

This past week at work was pleasant. Staff happily went about doing their tasks. Cherry's office was cleaned out. Catherine took her final box of things out on Friday.

Donna the LVN Instructor talked with me on Friday. She affirmed she was not leaving the school. She had suggestions for the Christmas Party. She wanted full staff participation. The Christmas

37

season was a good time for all to come together. I was so pleased to hear her words.

I interviewed Jean Stevenson RN for the Director's position. She was referred by Thelma Bledsoe, RN Advisors. The meeting lasted 2 hours. We discussed the school leadership style, my concerns regarding the program, the philosophy of the school, faculty, students, the future. We toured the Academy. She said she would pray, seek God's direction, and call me early next week. I know God will send what I have prayed for. I prayed for a leader who would support the philosophy of the school, pray with students and faculty, lead by example, have a positive relationship with Nursing Board, submit required documents on time without mistakes, a person with a presence of peace. God answers prayers.

The new changes with Margie back to Admissions and Priscilla to registrar has proved extremely beneficial. Margie has increased enrollment for the upcoming VP class from 17 to 32. She will have a minimum of 40 by 9/20/99. Matthew has been interviewing. A big help to the team.

We are on a new road paved by God. I feel wonderful.

Yesterday, Fatima Marianna Morris, my niece, married Robert Jackson in Los Angeles. They were married by her maternal Grandfather, Reverend Brooks. It was a wonderful time for all. All of her siblings were there. Karima, Kahled, Asei, Ade. Her mom, Fatu (Cassandra), looked great. Her dad, Ronnie, in tuxedo and tie, looked sophisticated. The grandmothers were beaming. They talked and laughed during the service at Rev. Brooks. He kept telling the young couple to look into each other's eyes, over and over.

On Thursday Mike, Greg, and I agreed to submit an offer for $1.6 million for the 1020 Washington, Colton. God will bless us. He will give the school the $160,000-$200,000 we will need to move. Lord, thank You. Thank You for Your guidance, my faith, my trust in You. For the staff, the school, the students, my family, my friends, my life to You. Thank You, Lord.

I have a peace beyond all understanding. I received an order for 100 books – Sadiq's from Rio Vista Elementary School. $558.00. First order of many to come. I submitted 3 poems, *Distant Land, Umuhoza, The Genie in the Bottle* to *Soul Vision*. All three will be submitted for review and recommendation for publication. On September 11th, Momma, all of Sadiq's kids, and I are flying to see him. God is good.

Aisha is back (1 week) from Campus Crusade Ocean City Project. God touched her life. She has transformed. I see and hear peace in her voice. She is blessed.

Tahira has been placed on Administrative Pay leave at Pomona Valley. She was caught up in another's misdoing. I placed a call on her behalf and her case was reviewed. She was so worried about losing everything. How could she? I talked to her about God's love for her. He would not allow her to lose anything; He had prepared her for this. He knows all things. I tried to spiritually encourage her as my father would do for me in my moments of despair. I advised her not to succumb to the world of sorrow, to see the best side of things, not to count her loss when she had not looked at what she had gained. An understanding of another's behavior. Ethics, being of good character. She retained her job. Her life goes on. I told her she was the fruit of my seed. I prayed to bear good fruit. I lived right, stay in God's blessing. I think of my fruit. God blessed us all.

My gratitude to Jesus...

9/6/99 ~ 8:58 a.m.

The Covenant with the Lord

The message yesterday at Church was Joshua 4:1-7. Leave the past behind. The story of Israelites needing to cross the Jordan River. Twelve men took 12 stones and took them from the Middle of the Jordan. The stones indicated where the water was cut off before the Ark of the Covenant of the Lord. The stones (12) were placed where the Israelites camped on the other side of the Jordan River.

I took the message as, "Look ahead, move forward. God has created a path for me." Remember from where I have come; know to where I am going. I have a covenant with the Lord, "Use my hands, Lord, and my feet. Use my heart. Lord, speak to me. You can do anything You want, just use me. He speaks to me. He uses me. He has a covenant with me." Thank You, Lord.

July 31, 1999 at 1:05 a.m. He called me by name. I rose, wrote, and worked as directed. He moves me.

9/8/99 ~ 7:33 a.m.

Jean Stevenson RN, MSN, accepted the Director of Nurses Position at $60,000/yr. She starts October 4, 1999. The owner of 1020 Washington accepted the offer of $1.6 million for the building. He will draw up the final plans. 60 days due diligence, 60 days reline the property, escrow to end 60-90 days for tenant improvements. Move by April 2000.

Lord, thank You.

Spoke with Jean Templeman about report due on Wednesday. She has not received adequate reports in numbers from Cherry and Nancy.

I will do my best with Donna Bostic's help. The staff continues to be quite busy. We had 11 DSD students – highest number in two years $3,300.00. Margie, Stephen, and Matthew are on the hustle to get 45 students in for the 9/20 VN Class.

Jolene fell at work today. She slipped in the lounge. Taken to SB Community Hospital via ambulance. Her words going out, "I'll be back tomorrow." I called her at home. She is okay. Sore. She'll be back Monday. Tomorrow, Momma, Jamila, Takara, Anwar, Jaise, and I are flying to Sacramento to see Sadiq. We are going to have a good time. Lord, thank You for Your protection. Mike said we should have the contract by Monday. I spoke with Otis today to inform him of the upcoming building purchase in Colton. April is coming fast.

Goodnight, Lord.

9/12/99 about 7:30 p.m.

Up in Vacaville, resting after two days of visiting Sadiq. The trip can be draining, the early flight with Momma and the four kids. Out on Friday 8:00 a.m. from Ontario. We arrived in Sacramento Airport at 9:00 a.m. Rented a car and drove to Vacaville, about 40 minutes. Signed into the hotel, unloaded, and stretched for two minutes. We went to Joe's Restaurant for breakfast. By 11:30, we were off to the Prison to see Sadiq. We arrived at 12:10. The doors do not open until 12:30. We were told to leave the premises. Off to a local am/pm lot until 12:40. Back to the Prison California Men Facility. We checked in and proceed through the line. Then, Takara's top is not acceptable. Her thick straps can be seen through her white sweater. I returned to the room for her to change. We returned to find Momma and the others waiting. She was not allowed to enter with the kids. They were listed under my name. I saw the disappointment in her face. She has not seen Wilbert, her baby, for 3-4 years. Now so close, she was forced to wait another hour. All cleared, we entered and waited another 20 minutes for Sadiq to enter the day room.

Eyes reddened, tears flowed. He embraced his daughter and me. After a brief hug, I directed him to the outside. There, his mother, Eula Mae Russ, waited to embrace him. What words can be spoken, many years of heartache, an embrace, a tear, and a smile. All is forgotten in that moment. She held her baby once again.

Sadiq continued to hug and kiss each of his children. Takara Russ age, Jamila Russ age 16, Anwar and Jaise Russ age 9. They were taller. He couldn't get over the appearance of the girls, no longer babies. His offspring. The day was filled with love, kisses, private handholding, walks, and conversation with each child. I wonder what kind of father he would have been if he had not been incarcerated?

On Sunday, we repeated the trip up at 6:30, out by 7:15. We arrived at the door at 7:50. Sadiq's friend, Lorraine, was there waiting. She had #4. Once inside, Takara's name did not appear on the list of my kids. Back to the room for the birth certificate. Momma had to change her top. In by 9:50 a.m. The day was going to be long. We played, ate, talked, laughed. I looked at Sadiq's face. I can see Daddy and David Jr. (his uncle). Such resemblance. By 3:00 p.m. it was time for us to leave. The girls got one last lecture from dad. We hugged, said 'I love you.' The door and gate closed behind us.

A trip worth making. Momma, at 75, is traveling better than all of us. She has strength and stamina. No complaints.

Resting in bed, she relaxed for the flight home. Already packed.

I sit in the tub, reflecting on the weekend and gave praise to God. Thank You, Lord, for another opportunity to see my brother.

Home tomorrow by 8:50 a.m.

9/12/99 ~ 11:41 a.m.

Home. We arrived at Ontario Airport at 10:00 a.m. Greeted by Linda, Jamila's mom. I came home to my honey. House clean. Welcomed with a warm hug and extended kiss! Oh yeah! Home alone, Aisha is in Moro Bay with friends. Oh yeah.

9/15/99 ~ 6:48 a.m.

God guides us daily. I have been working with the LVN Team to address the needs of the program. Schedules, records, orientation for new staff. Addressing Jean's recommendations. The temperament of the school is positive. We are working as a team. Margie and Stephen have been hustling to enroll 45 students for Monday! It is a new day at the school. I have issued memos to address grades and absenteeism. We move forward! "The fear of the Lord is in the Foundation of happiness." Pastor Dollars' message, understanding God's will and purpose for my life. He would not have commissioned me to do Four-D Success Academy and not equipped me to succeed.

As I move through life, I reflect on my travels. God has protected me, carried me, been in front of me, behind me. He has forgiven me 100 times over for my sins, even those that I repeated. He forgave me. I have gained strength, knowledge, wisdom, and fear of the Lord's power. Love of the Lord, understanding, happiness for life, consideration of others, and peace.

I have been extremely blessed by my Lord.

Today, I attend the Director of Nurses Meeting in Pasadena. All is well.

Today, I should receive the contact to sign for the building. Lord, I have prayed for this, the Child Care Center. I will follow, lead me, and use me. Thank You.

Love, Your Child, Linda

9/20/99 ~ 7:30 a.m.

Today is my father's Birthday. His life on this earth would have been 75 years. Daddy has been gone 5 years. I miss him so, but His spirit lives with me.

I have not received the contract for the buildings yet. Today, we start a new VN class. I expect 40-45 students. Class starts at 8:30 a.m. I must go now, it is 7:35 a.m. I will be back this evening to write.

Well, I am back. I left the office at 8:15 p.m. for home. What a day. The new class of VN is at 38 students. Faculty and I explained attendance policy. We will see who is left in 30 days.

I interviewed 3 nurses. I am seeking faculty for the CNA and VN Program. I counseled and placed 8 students on probation for either attendance or academic poor performance.

Then I dismissed Millie, a new person who Cherry hired as Asst. Director of Nurses. She did not qualify for the position. Mille wanted to work 8-5, unable to do clinical due to child care problems. (I was told today the child care was a "healthy" 15 year old female). She was taking this young girl to a babysitter before school at 5:30 a.m. She had requested that I change the clinical schedule to allow her to arrive at 8:00 a.m. Too many complications foreseen. Terminated.

Home, happy to be here, mentally exhausted. I am in bed after a long shower and foot rub.

Happy Birthday, Daddy. Thank you for the spiritual lift. Tomorrow, I go see the twins. Momma called to say the grades are slipping.

9/22/99 ~ 9:50 p.m.

We admitted 41 students into the VN Class, 5 into the Pharmacy Tech, and 4 into the Medical Biller Program. The Cont. Ed has been going better. The staff is working hard. We are tired, but moving forward. I have the contract for review $1.6 million. I will sign and return with $10,000. I know God is preparing us for the future.

Charlie is doing better. He says he never was hurting, just tired. He truly had painted himself into a corner. Charlotte, his daughter, is the new CEO of Adopt-a-Bike/Computer.

It's now 10:00 p.m. I will sing Amazing Grace and go to sleep.

Goodnight, Lord.

9/25/99 ~ 10:28

Today, I participated in the NCNW Walk a Thon for the Bethune Center. We raised $700.00. I am mentally and physically tired. I went by Charles'. He was with Charlotte, Sylvester, Jean, were there with the tutors and kids. I spoke to him, he sounded tired, and I listened to his breathing. I pray that he rebounds to excellent health. I got tearful, and then I stopped. This is Charlie. We have spent hours talking about beliefs of science of mind. Denies false evidence. There is no illness. It's only believed in the mind, false evidence. I think positive, positive flow of spirits. At 3:15 while sitting on my floor, I feel a chill. Charlie was on my mind. False evidence, he is okay. At 80 years old, loved by me and a host of hundreds, he claims good health. Unshaken visually. I know. I hear it in his voice. Something has happened. He was like this after the bike-a-thon held at the Air force base in 1997. He literally put it together in 3½ months. He ran himself down and he recovered. This is the last time of pushing himself into a corner.

Lord, You know my heart.

Take care of my friend, Charlie.

9/26/99 ~ 10:07

I spoke with Charlie today. He's at home in PJ's. He sounds tired, low energy. He has no pain. His breathing is short. I have noticed perched lip breathing the past year. His lungs are involved. I thought he possibly had a stroke. Two weeks ago, I stopped by his office. I had him to squeeze my hands. He had equal strength, no facial distortion, but he was not moving his facial muscles. Possible slight stroke. Gait steady. Appetite diminished. Stated he had lost six pounds. I could see the loss in his face.

We laughed and talked for a while. I last saw Charlie on Tuesday 9/21/99. Charlie was my mentor. He had guided me through my worst difficult times with the school and my personal life. He was (is) a true friend. I have prayed for his physical healing and full strength. Charlie loves the kids like no other. God, there is no one to take his place. Keep him with us. The kids need Charlie. His desires are unmatched by another. His spirit is pure, his love of God unyielding. His teaching is unselfish. His direction is unmatched. His love is all he gives.

Thank You for answering my prayers.

9/28/99 ~ 10:22 p.m.

Trials continue to come. Victory is mine. Loaded with work, VN reports, seeking clinical facilities, ABHES report, finances, CNA Program, disciplinary issues. Meeting with the VN faculty to discuss the program, student status. Five minutes into the meeting, two instructors, Betty and Jolene, voiced their strong opinion of my decision and how I handled the VN students. My position was firm. I will not lower standards, students were going to come or be dismissed. Grades per Module must be 75%. Betty, who voiced, "You can fire me if you want to," wishes to resign. The school will go on. That was made clear to her.

I know in my heart that the students are not prepared to move forward. Statistically, 40% would fail their boards.

God already knows the outcome. He prepares the path before me, Four-D Success Academy. Protect and guide us, Lord. A new day is ahead. I face it with all of my energy and love to make a positive difference in someone's life.

Today, I faxed the signed agreement paper for 1020 Washington to Mike B. We should be in Escrow within 10 days. Nervous, but joyful.

9/30/09 ~ 5:54 a.m.

If I hold my peace, the Lord will fight my battles! At the staff meeting, Betty and Jolene were insolent and disrespectful. Replacement of both is in the making. I need additional staff members. I will change the climate to positivity. Lord, thank You for another day.

We got Parkview Hospital!

9/30/99 ~ 10:34 p.m.

I typed the letters (memos) to Jolene and Betty, clearly expressing my thoughts and actions to be taken if infractions were repeated. I spoke with Jolene about her comments. She acknowledged she was fired up and someone had pointed out the statement for her response. Item resolved. I will speak with Betty tomorrow.

Good meeting with Greg Sheet CPA and staff budget, drops, admissions, audits, grades, team work.

Charlie is still out. He will never say he is sick. It does not compute. He is just out. I miss him.

10/2/99 ~ 2:00 p.m.

Business and Professional Women Presentation

I had received an invitation to be the guest speaker at the Fall Conference of the Business and Professional Women Organization. I had invited my mother but being away from her boys from Friday through Sunday was too much. She could have brought them. But that's okay, I understand.

Momma Vivian, Jeanie, Andre, Walter III, and Ernell came. Not to hear me, but to spend the weekend in Laughlin-Colorado Bell-Casino, Nevada. Up at 7:30 a.m. I prepare myself. I don't write speeches, but I had reviewed their points of interest. The topic, "Risky Business: An Entrepreneur Approach To Small Business Management." I had one hour and fifteen minutes. Dressed in a new violet two-piece suit, I was ready. As I took each step down the hall leading to the entrance door, my heart started to pound. But wait, what is there to be afraid of? The pounding would cease. I enter the conference room. Greeted. Once I said my name, the lady at the door said, "You're our guest speaker?" I smiled and said, "Yes."

At 10:00 a.m. I was at the Podium "Through God, all things are possible." I spoke from my heart. God guided my words. I hope the speech was well-received. I finished at 11:15. Congratulations were given. I engaged in a lovely lunch and said my goodbyes. Sitting here alone in my room, I reflect on what I said. My words had value, meaning. I was here. I was told I spoke of words that help others. I am blessed. God is good, all the time. With God, all things are possible.

Lord, thank You.

10/7/99

"Key Her Car"

On October 4th, Jean Stevenson MHA, RN started as Director of Nurses. She has a calming spirit. Very knowledgeable, systematic in process. She called a meeting on Wednesday 10/6/99 at 10:00 a.m. to meet the VN staff. I called Jolene to ask about the class 8 schedules to inform her of the Wednesday meeting. While on the telephone, I told her of the comment by an instructor to "key my car." I told her I did not know who the instructor was. I did not understand the hatred for me. I desire to help others, and the 'role model,' 'the teacher,' who should express kindness and compassion, is suggesting to students to key my car. I hung up.

Ten minutes later, Jolene called to confess she made the statement. Not to incite damage. She was angry over me dismissing Cherry Houston and placing the students on probation. I asked what did she intended for the students to do? Why even suggest a thing? She said she didn't mean it; that's why she was sorry. I informed her Cherry resigned. She said Cherry said I fired her. Jolene seems not to want to accept my answer.

I was visited by a student in class 7. She reports Jolene gave the students the answer to the neurological test, she suggested the keying of my car, wrote the member of State Office on the board, and told the class to report me. Today, I received an urgent call from another student. She told me Jolene, Betty, and Donna "want my head on a platter." The student caller informed me Ms. Christopherson suggested the keying of my car and if anyone knew where she (me) lived, maybe someone could toilet paper her house? She also stated Ms. C gave the word for word answer to the neurological test and allowed students to act out and come and go. No control in class. Ms. Hansen is having a hard time trying to undue 8 months of damage.

Betty told students she had spoken with Cherry. Cherry gave her the number to the State Office and told her to tell the students to report me for disciplinary action. She let students out at 7:00 p.m. from Clinicals. Donna had 10 to 14 students failing. She gave Care Plans as credit to boost grade.

Sitting in my office, I was/am overwhelmed with grief. I left my office for a walk. I walked and sang out loud, "Lead me, guide me." I sang loud and wiped away the tears. I sang loud to sooth my soul. I sang loud and asked God to lead me. I sang loud for peace and understanding. I sang loud unto the Lord. Lead me, guide me along the way. For if You lead me, I cannot stray. Lord, let me walk each day with thee. Lead me, oh Lord, lead me. I am weak and I need the strength and power to help me over the weakest hour. Help me through my darkness. I pray to thee. Lead me, oh Lord, lead me. My song of peace – peace for my soul to dry my tears. I so much want the students to succeed. It is an uphill struggle. Lead me.

I am tired. I rose at 4:00 a.m. At work before 5:00 a.m. At home this evening at 7:00 p.m. I am mentally tired. Tomorrow is another day. I press on.

Thank You, Lord.

10/8/99 ~ 9:50 p.m.

Reality. Enemies are within. I received a letter from a student. She reports the unethical actions of the past Director (Houston) and instructors Donna, Jolene, and Betty D. Cheating – giving students answers to the final and Neurological test. Passing students with F grades by giving credit for Care Plans. Encouraging students to key my car and follow me home to find out where I live. The implied threat was personal. I called the attorney Richard Nevins. I left a message for him to call me on Monday. I informed Charlie Seymour, Chair of Advisory Board, of the letter. He kept a copy. I discussed my actions, and I listened to his advice. I presented the letter to Ernell, my husband. His response was, "Don't they know they can get hurt if they come here?" I am his wife. He will not let any harm come to me. We discussed the events, my response. Monday, Jolene will be dismissed, and I will talk with the students. I placed a call to Charlie. I am seeking Tom or Lillie Rivera. I would like for either to come and speak to the students. Another voice, another perspective may save one. They don't know how much the instructors have set them up to fail.

I will press on. God is ALWAYS PRESENT.

Tonight, I am secure. I shall sleep a peaceful night.

Thank You, Lord.

10/9/99 ~ 9:05 p.m.

I tossed and turned through the night. My spirit was restless. How do I save the students? I don't fear for myself, my family, my passion for the school. I am most concerned with the deliberate misguidance the students have received. God will guide my path.

Tahira visited with her dog Cleo (Cleopatra) a pit-bull and chow mixed. I was surprised at how cute she was. I am over the dog issue. Off to get my nails done. I ended up at Carmen's on Foothill. Looking for a Nailologist, I met Yvonne Almos. She did an excellent job. No cuts. Foot massage with oatmeal and honey based cream. Wonderful. Too tired to go to Charlene's for the appreciation lunch. I returned home to read *The Mother Church*, a Christian Science book Charlie had given me. I can relate to the stories of the process to build an extension to the Mother Church, What cannot God do? Nothing! I think of the students, the cruelty of the staff, and I shed tears. Weeping no more, God tells me to call Tom and Lillie Rivera, Professors at Redlands University and Cal State San Bernardino. I explain what has happened. I seek their support to give the students better direction and get them back on track.

They agreed. Lillie is coming Tuesday a.m. at 8:30 a.m. Lord, thank You.

I returned to reading. Press forward. "There is no power that can separate me from God."

10/11/99 ~ 12:25 a.m.

Monday morning, lying here alone in my room, I prepare for God. The quietness of the house is peaceful. Aisha is in her room. Ernell is asleep in the Den. The rotating fan spreads a cool breeze in the room. I relax, re-read and underline a few pages in *The Mother Extension Church*.

I woke up by 6:30 a.m. Aisha and I went to the 7:30 a.m. Church service. The lesson was on Matthew 16: 13 "Who do you say I am?" The question Jesus asked the disciples. Who do I think He is? The one who is always present. He leads me and guides me. A pleasant day at home. I washed a few loads and worked on letters to ABHES and the Nursing Board regarding the current situation at Four-D Success Academy.

Ernell barbecued ribs, chicken, roasted corn on the cob, sweet potatoes, and rolls. I steamed a bunch of green beans, fixed our plates, and enjoyed a good tasty meal. Being home with him is very good for me. I have his love and protection. I have peace.

Tomorrow, we'll see changes at the school. I pray the students act responsible to their education and not react to the dismissal of faculty. I have their best interest in mind. The Lord will/is protect/ing us. Applications to the Bureau and ABHES are up for review. Lord, let the reviewers find favor in us. Goodnight, Lord.

10/11/99 ~ 10:30 p.m.

I dismissed Jolene, R.N. because of unethical acts. She gave students the answers to the neurological test. I spoke with class 7 about all that concerned me. Keying my car, following me home, toilet papering my home, cheating on tests, observations, calling the state agencies. I informed the students I did call the state and the

Nursing Board to report their issues. A letter was written to both. Most students appreciated the change. Ms. Jean Stevenson, the new Director, is arriving. What changes must be done?

Lord, thank You.

10/15/99 ~ 10:48

I have seen the difference in Donna's attitude this week. She has popped her head into my office to inform me of student's attendance. She called Kaye to plead her position. She is worried about being terminated. The jury is still out on her. I have some questions about her grade book.

I spoke with Stephen on Wednesday. I did his evaluation. The request for his evaluation came on the heel of my statement at the management meeting. He is asking for $40/hr. from $28/hr. It may be time for him to move on. He was hired to do a job. His salary of $28/hr. is comparable to Adm. at the local University. The maximum will be $60,000.

Jean Stevenson and I had a meeting with Jean Templeman in Sacramento. The DON orientation went well. Things will work out. Home with Ernell, I am tired.

I will press on – develop plans – set goals – press on. I saw Supervisor Gerry Eaves at the Sacramento Airport. I spoke with him, asking for his support on my loan for $1.2 million to relocate the school. He said he would talk with Tom Larkin. Thanks, Lord.

10/16/99 ~ 8:26 a.m.

Awakened with Stephen on my mind, his actions to move his income up, his statement that I pay the men less. Will he speak to

Michael Williams to stir the pot? It would be the end of his employment.

My spirit is stirred. I called Mona. Press on! I can't drop the ball. Open another site, God knows what I want to do. I should not sit still. The Child Care Center, call Ray Anday to view and measure the site. Write the proposal to Jane Adams. Get busy.

This past month has been heavy. I managed to press on with God's helping hand. My family (Ernell especially) is always with me.

There is much to do, but I (we) can do it.

A new day – call my momma. Said hello and I love you.

Eula stays busy. I catch her when I can. She is doing well.

The boys are at Charlie's study session.

10/21/99

It doesn't seem so long since I've written my thoughts. I have been tired. Up early, I have awakened as early as 3:00 a.m. Tossed and turned, thinking and praying. Drifting back to sleep. Reawakened at 5:00 a.m. The alarm goes off at 5:30 a.m. My goal is to rise and dress for work and get to the office by 6:45 a.m. The quiet time is my prayer time, my quiet time. Time to reflect, think, breathe slowly, deeply. Move forward. Stephen's action to cross out his title "Business Development" irritated me to no end. I found his action disrespectful and petty. I know how Juanita feels when she tries to talk to him. He is never satisfied. His salary is now $62,400. Greg says he is worth it. But if aggravated, I would not keep him.

I seek peace at Four-D. After dealing with Cherry, the students, and Jolene, I am not in the mood for nonsense. I talked with Charlie. He helped me to focus. Can he do the job? Yes. "Then don't try to sift gnats and swollen camels!" I eased the stress load. No camels for me. I press on.

I met with David. We discussed the preliminary drawings for the building. Mike said he will receive the contract by next Tuesday. We move on. Lord, thanks a million.

10/26/99

Today is Tuesday, and I had a full day. Especially after yesterday. Well, on Monday, Wendy and I attended the BPPVE Annual Report in-service. She is preparing the 3-year report. After receiving her info, she left. I stayed to hear about the "New calculation fee." Up to a 200-300% increase in fees based on gross income. From $4,725 to $12,500 - $20,000. This is ridiculous. I will rewrite a letter to the BPPVE in protest.

I arrived at Mona Houston's home in Oceanside at 10:30 a.m. She has a lovely, comfortable 2-story home with a yappy dog. After a tour, breakfast, eggs, muffins, bacon, coffee and OJ, we headed out. We had looked in the yellow papers to locate local schools, searched the Internet to view web pages.

Off to check out a couple of school sites. Mercie College was gone. Career Technical College, open 6 months, was in place. Another college (Voc. Ed) was gone. There were less than 10 schools in the area. 2 VN 2 Med Biller. Room for us. We then went to Camp Pendleton. It is huge, over 37,000 service men and 50,000 family members. It is a "city." Everything, stores, fast food, furniture stores, school, a city. We met with Dennis Sherrod - Education Department. I will send him a package. I met with Colonel Smith Sect. Rhonda. Call by Thursday for telephone meeting. Spoke with

Colonel Gill at the Hospital. Seeking clinical site. Open to 3-11 rotation. I must call Tri City Hospital for possible clinical site. We put in a day's work. Ended at 6:30 p.m. Had dinner at Outback until 8:45 p.m. It was great spending time with Mona. She is a thinker. No pressures from her. She gives her time, no mention of compensation. We discuss strategy, moves, and contracts. Home at 10:36 p.m. Smooth sailing on the 5N. Cruise control set at 74 miles/hr. I guide the car home.

Sleepy, tired, I am blessed. The road is lit by God. I must travel it. Everything will work out. The building is coming. I realize April 2000 is 6 months away. The Lord must guide this project to closure. He knows I need $200,000. He will provide.

Goodnight, Jesus.

11/2/99

I signed the contract to purchase 1020 Washington, Colton for $1,600,000. I expect the TI to be about $386,000. So Lord, I need $190,000 for the portion I owe. You know what I don't have! I know things will work out. I am excited as I see God's works. The building and furniture are to come from San Bernardino Community Hospital. I envision the building, room, office with furniture, Child Care and Children, oh yes! I spoke with Richard Nevins, Attorney. He will do the papers for the Child Care - Umuhoza. One day there will be children at Four-D Success Academy School.

I spoke with Donald Brown in New York. The scripture about the piece "Middle Passage." As we spoke, we began to talk about health and Education in Africa. He has been traveling extensively to South Africa. I informed him of my continued interest. He suggested I send info on my goals, plans, and cost. He is involved in a funding project and may have connections. All things are possible through God. I informed Stephen of the possibilities of receiving financial support for work in Uganda.

Stephen informed me the President of Uganda will be here in February 2000, and I will have the opportunity to meet him. I think of where God has brought the school and I cry. We have come far.

I am thinking of Friends of Four-D Success. Cherry will not have input in the company. She tells others she is President, but I still hold the office until I am voted out. That will not happen. On November 7th, we will vote on the new officers.

Life goes on. God protects us. I have continued to address the negativity of the school image from the students associated with the destruction and faculty problems. We have moved forward. Good things are ahead. Thank You, Lord.

11/9/99 ~ 10:30 p.m.

On November 7, 1999, the business for Friends of Four-D Success Academy was attended to. By-laws were amended. I was voted into CEO position, Donna Bostic voted into Secretary Position, Ernell Smith voted into CFO position, Jennifer Singleton was voted in as a member, and Cherry Houston was voted out of the organization in the best interest of the company.

We continued to address the complaints of the students. Most are of no value other than a few who want to keep mess going. I can't wait for class 7 to be gone. A nightmare with a happy ending and Jean is addressing the staffing issues, curricular changes, and planning for the future. We need (must) bring our numbers up for the Feb class. I know God will provide. He always has. All programs will continue to flourish.

I am marketing the school and myself. Wendy is submitting info on our performance to several groups for possible recognition.

Project Jamal is progressing. Margaret has provided me with a very good initial proposal. Our goal is to do a public TV announcement with LL Cool J or likeness to encourage young African-American males to buckle up. This could be a national program. I have not given any attention to revising the Child Care budget. I know I must focus on it to have the opportunity to qualify for funds. I know the Child Care Center will greatly improve some of the students' situations. Lord, open me up to do more. At times, I am not doing enough. Productivity lower than normal. I have been feeling mentally exhausted, my physical stamina is low. I am sleepy, so goodnight all.

11/9/99

Today, Ernell and I signed the Escrow Papers on 1020 West Washington Ave. Colton 92324. The feeling was exciting, concerning, apprehensive, and not fearful. Now Lord, we need the money. I later called Juanita and Steven into my office to explain the process. I needed their help to monitor cash flow. Ernell and I had taken a second on our home and he would pull his retirement to raise $100,000. But we needed $100,000 more. Every effort will be put forth to press on. I know God has a bright future for all of us. This morning, Margie was at the office at 7:30 a.m. working. She and I talked about the school. She suggested we pray at the potluck for the school on the day before Thanksgiving. I asked Mary Salim if she would ask Pastor John to come and speak. God is in Four-D Success. He protects us and blesses us. The past year, I have seen the change in the school. Staff, lack of support from several members sabotaged the spirit of the school. Some instructors portrayed student by having them to believe they were A+ students when, in fact, they lack significant knowledge and skills. They have been set up to fail. We have tried to assist all of them. Of the 20 students, only 6 will accept our continued assistance. We will continue to improve on all aspects of the school.

We will make it. I pray to receive equipment, furniture, from SB Community Hospital to fill the new school.

Thank You, Lord.

11/15/99 ~ 10:24 p.m.

Sadiq called today, cheerful. I could see the big smile over the telephone. He is aware of his son's trouble in school. Auntie is on them. He is grateful for my involvement.

We made another pay period. I had to transfer $45,000 from the business savings, leaving $5,377.70 in the account. I reflected on the low account. Bills due. The loan needed to complete Escrow. Student enrollment is low. I don't know if it's due to the holiday season. I can't get anxious, fearful. God has brought me/Four-D this far. He will not leave us now. I don't know where the money will come for the building. I don't have $190,000 - my percent of the $1,985,000. Lord, I seek your help today as I do daily. I received the lease and operation cost on the building. The corporate tax paper on Four-D shows $84,000 net. I have to inquire from Greg about the initial amount of $174,000. A $90,000 adjustment is a BIG adjustment. I don't know what to expect. But God does. Goodnight, Lord.

The evilness of the instructors separated from the school runs deep. Jolene, Nancy, and Betty have made false allegations against the school. As I read the comments, I thought how foolish of them. The very things they report are the areas of which they were responsible. They are not aware of the written document, which I submitted to the Nursing Board in September. Their goal is to harm the school and me.

I know God has me and the school protected. It is disheartening to experience hatred. I know Cherry is knowingly involved in their actions. I pray that my actions to protect the school and myself are not, nor do they develop into negative reactions.

While standing in my kitchen, tears swelled in my eyes. Overcome with my thoughts of the school, the students, my goals, and desires for their success and the attack of the enemy. I fought back the tears. I will not succumb to their hate. The school will not be disrupted by callous madness and discard. I am a child of God. I have a spiritual covenant with Him. I know that my God prevails above all others. In His kingdom is Four-D Success Academy. In His kingdom are security, peace, love, kindness and caring. I live in the kingdom. I seek continued peace, calm, and love. I express myself through actions, not negative reactions. I am loved. I am the chosen one. I am the President/CEO. I am the one who was called by name at 1:05 a.m. on July 31, 1991. I am HIS child and the Enemy will not prevail. Heavenly Father, cast out ALL who rise against me. Give me victory; give the Academy victory above all others.

- Students having a verbal confrontation at the hospital – new region.
- Students failing test.
- Students not willing to help each other.
- Students not praying together.
- Bring the prayer back.

Lord, thank You. Your Child, Linda

11/22/99 ~ 10:25 p.m.

I spoke with Richard Nevins, Attorney as an Advisor to the Academy. Informed of the letter from the Nursing Board, the six alleged items against the school reported by Nancy and Betty, and my discussion with Charlie Seymour Board Advisor. An injunction against using the school list and students to teach materials offered by the school. I am requesting he send the letter for more impact. My whole day was consumed with students' issues. Six students walked out of Kaye's class and went to another school for interviews and were tested. They returned to talk with me. We met for 30-40 minutes. At the end, two students destroyed the school's admission papers. Tomorrow, I will know if they return to Four-D.

I shared as much as I could about the efforts to destroy the school. I can't be broken. My spirit can't be touched. So they try to destroy the students, take them away hoping the school will closed. I am saddened beyond words, but I know God is carrying the school and me. My faith is stronger than they think! God will provide for us at Four-D Success Academy. We are His property. And no distractions will come to us. I pray to be a better manager of His business. I pray for Him to speak to me, tell me what to do next.

I cancelled my trip to Washington. I can't afford to leave for 7 days. 2nd step in the right direction – the 1st was talking to Richard.

Lord, thank You for the lessons in life.

The minister said Sunday that life is a job. The job of life is to decipher facts during the crisis. Each crisis has been different and significant. Rewritten program (CNA), staff strategy, financial shortage, lies against the business and false allegations. I forget about the building, the pursuit for loans. I must contact Delores with EDA and Rosina with Union Bank.

Lord, I am glad You are in my corner.

Night, Lord.

11/23/99 ~ 6:57 a.m.

Bring the Prayer Back to Class!

On Monday night, I laid in bed praying, "Lord, what do I do? Where do I go? The enemy is plentiful." I laid there and silently listened, "Fight back." But the fight is not a physical one. It is a spiritual one. I knew at that moment what I needed to do. Visit each class and pray. I arrived to school and went into classroom 4. Without stopping, no intro directions, I said, "Those who wish to stand and pray, please do so. Those who choose not to, remain seated." I prayed for them, their success, their understanding. I prayed for peace, kindness, and calmness.

After the prayer, I informed them of the purpose of Four-D Success Academy, how they have been used by people who want to close the school. The ones who have lodged a complaint against me know they can't break my spirit. Therefore, they have involved the students – don't pay your loans. They don't care if your personal credit is destroyed, as long as the school (or me) is hurt. I explain Donna Bostic's (consultant) CUP Theory. A cup turned upside-down cannot be filled, no matter what. They had become inverted and I needed them to upright themselves. Allow us to teach them.

I progress to the 3 other classes with the same message.

I spoke with Samuel Teo, the new class instructor. We discussed the freedom to pray. I encouraged him to pray with the students before the start of class. He was pleased to hear that. Samuel went to class and prayed with his students.

Prayer is powerful. It lifts, it binds, and it heals.

After speaking and praying with the students and faculty, I proceeded to gather the materials for the alleged statements to the Nursing Board.

Today, we are having a potluck and baby shower for Aja. Mary Salim's. Pastor John will attend to pray up the school, staff, and students.

The Lord continues to bless us and protect us.

Thank You, Lord. Your Child, Linda

11/23/99 ~ 10:54 p.m.

What a blessed day!

A day for fellowship and thanksgiving. The day was filled with laughter and lightness of spirit. Festive! Potluck! The staff had "set" the tables in the conference room. The tables were covered with white tablecloths with a floral centerpiece, food covering every inch.

Pastor John and Kathy graced our presence with words of encouragement and prayer. It was a blessed day. We feasted and we spoke of faith and God's goodness. The spirit was present.

We followed the luncheon with Aja's baby shower. Gifts, gifts, gifts, joy in the house. We did a "baby due" date game. Aja is due January 5, 2000. I selected 2, 4, and 7.

Aisha was present for the baby shower. She was well-received. Aisha has been missed. The staff meeting started at 3:20. Usual business, but then we each say words of thanks. The emotions were let loose, tears flowed, words of thankfulness for the life of a child. These were expressions of thankfulness for husbands, kids. Thankfulness for the philosophy, mission vision of the school. Thankfulness for daily delivery, safe passage. Thankfulness for coming to Four-D for employment, thankfulness to God for my mother, for her giving of love. That kept the school's door open. We were being healed. God is present in Four-D Success Academy. I know we will continue to climb the mountain and God is holding the safety line.

Lord, I thank You for letting me see another day, for giving me the opportunity one more time to help someone else. Lord, I thank You. I called my mother before leaving work to tell her I loved her. She could feel it coming. She has a way of trying to change the subject, but I got it out. "Momma, I love you!" Night, Lord.

11/24/99 ~ 10:57 p.m.

Thanksgiving Day.

Walter Jr. said the blessing. Tahira, Aisha, and I thought it was Daddy reincarnated. He went on and on.

Awakened at 5:00 a.m. I laid in bed and prayed. I thought about the false allegations. I need to write a letter to Jean Templeman, Nurse Consultant. Lord, I was misled. I think of yesterday. A good day! I rose at 5:30 a.m., entered my office, and began my report. I stopped working at 11:02 a.m.

Time to prepare for the feast, visit with family. We met Tahira at Momma Vivian's house. Walter Jr. called and told me he was coming with Fatima, Robert, and baby. Their wedding pictures were gorgeous.

I visited Momma, and the boys hung out with Tahira and Aisha. We talked, laughed, and ate German Chocolate Cake.

Home, in bed, relaxing. Lord, I have so much I am thankful for.

Donna Bostic called to say Happy Thanksgiving to her best friend. I was on the list.

Goodnight, Lord.

11/26/99 ~ 6:53 a.m.

Yesterday, I sat alone at home for most of the day. Aisha went shopping and Ernell went to Momma's house to fix commodes. As I sat in the family room, I relaxed and took in the view of the backyard. The house was peaceful. I thought to myself, "I like this, a clean house, a good life, alone to relax." After watching Judge Mills on TV, I rose to work on my report to Jean Templeman.

I felt full, overwhelmed. I stood at the window of my office, looking out over the trees, up to the crest of the mountains, I began to pray. My heart was full of sorrow. The students have suffered so much. They have lost so much. The tears flowed. How could they have such hate to destroy the students and the school, to hurt me? I was reduced to heart pain, tears of sadness, as I thought of their actions and lies.

Lord, how could they hurt the students? We were to make a positive difference in their lives.

I prayed for an answer, for strength, for guidance, for protection against all enemies. I prayed the Nursing Board would continue the privileges of the school.

I would be delighted.

I sat down to the computer at 1:30 p.m. I rose at 10:29 p.m. I found Ernell lying on the couch in the den, watching TV. I made myself a tall glass of hot tea, and cleaned the kitchen before sitting down with him for an hour before we retired for the evening.

Today, I rise in the presence of God. My spirit is quiet, not in turmoil.

Ernell is preparing to go bike riding with Steven. I am on my way to Evette's hair salon. I return home ready to continue to complete the report to Jean and start a new project.

Lord Jesus, thank You.

11/28/99 ~ 9:55 p.m.

Today is Sunday. I attended Church with Aisha. She woke me up asking, "Are you going to Church? I'll be back in 15 minutes." She was. I was reviewing last week's message. Luke 8:22. The crisis. The faith.

Ernell and I went to the movies. We saw 'The Last Days' and 'The Bone Collector.' We joked about being together so much. This could become catchy.

Tonight, I watched 'Touched by an Angel.' The message of God's blessing... bring prayer and praise back into the place of business. God answers prayers. The environment started with prayer, should continue with prayer. I listened to the message, the songs of praise. I felt as though God was talking to me. The message was clear. Keep praying.

I envisioned the classroom of class 7. I prayed for each chair and the body that sits there. I prayed for an open mind. I prayed that God would show us what to do. I bathed in His love and protection.

Lord, thank You.

11/31/99 ~ 6:52 a.m.

Answering the allegations is tiring. After spending 15 hours writing my responses, I met with Richard Nevins, Attorney, yesterday at 2:00 p.m. He reviewed, made changes with the eyes of an attorney. Four hours later, I had a rough draft to redo. I hadn't eaten all day. Now, I had another 3 hours of work. I arrived back at Four-D to pick up the disk Wendy had copied the original onto, grabbed a bit from Carl's Jr., and hit the freeway. Home by 8:00 p.m. Upon arriving home, I kissed (pecked) Ernell and explained what I had to do and I was off to my office from 8:45 p.m. to 11:45. I read and revised as discussed with Richard.

I awakened this a.m. at 5:55 with prayer on my mind. I am asking Jesus for guidance, for protection. I think of all I need to do. I rise.

Have a blessed day in Jesus.

12/1/99 ~ 6:55 p.m.

This job ain't easy. But if it was, everyone would be doing it. Today, R. Fleming, VN student, came in today to drop from the program.

No problem. But, she came with her mother. She requested her transcript. I had to review Jolene's record book. We located the final grades for Module 2. She failed 2 subjects, pharmacology and nutrition. She had probation in Module 3 and had to repeat Module 3 for absence. She missed 22 days.

Now, she and her mother want to argue how she could have received 2 F's when she had straight A's in the 1st Module. They did not seem to relate 22 days out probation as probable reasons for failing the subjects. Sometimes, dealing with ignorance is tiring and frustrating. Mother and daughter, two grown women.

I had to tell the student, if she thought she was going to disrespect me in my office, she could have a seat in the lobby and I would speak with her mother. Mistake! She and child are the same. I move on! I am trying to make contact with Delores. 3 days, no returned call. Call placed to Dwight Morton with SB Community Hospital for equipment.

Home, showered, and ready for bed at 6:05 p.m. Visited with Ernell.

Lord, thanks.

12/2/99 ~ 10:47 p.m.

I awakened at 5:30 a.m., rose, and prepared to work in my office. I had mail, mail, mail. By 7:30, I had read, sorted, discarded, and re-filed all the mail. I decided to stay home and continued to work. I complete the review of the Personnel and Student Catalog. By 3:00, I was done with the catalogs. I washed a couple of loads of clothes, made out the bills, then cooked dinner. I decided to attend Weight Watchers. Yes, it is time. I feel fat. The grey hair just isn't the same on this overweight body. I had wondered what I would look like at

200 lbs. Well, I weigh 194.2 lbs., that's close enough. So here I go, down at least 50 lbs. I started gaining the weight 5 years ago when Daddy died. Initially, I gained 10-12 lbs. (from 158-170). Then, I gradually gained additional pounds during my troubled marriage years. The last 10-15 occurred in the last 6 months. The situation at the school has me solemnly saddened.

Jean Stevenson called me tonight at about 8:00 p.m. Class 8 with 21 students, eleven failing the Module. We discussed options to aid the students. They will be given the option to attend Wednesday class for the term, or drop. Four-D owes them the opportunity to make it.

I sit and reflect on Cherry's words of jealousy. Was she determined to destroy me by hurting the students? Destroy the school? Did she collaborate with Nancy, Jolene, and Betty to hurt the school and me? I believe she said, I remember Cherry saying, "You're Four-D and Four-D is you. Destroy one, the other will perish."

I sit in the chair and tears swell behind my eyelids. My head throbs, my mind is jumbled. Why is their hatred so deep to destroy all that they couldn't control? The students had been given A, A+ throughout Module 1. They actually earned 60-65% for extra credit. This would raise their grade to 90%. Fatal false grades. False hope to individuals used to "getting over." It all backfired.

I cry and pray. Lord, I can only depend on You. I can't allow negative thoughts to enter my spiritual being. The school will continue. God's vision will succeed! The guiding light will shine brighter.

I pray for peace in my heart. I thank God for His blessing. I thank God for Four-D Success Academy. I thank God for selecting me.

I spoke with Rosina today. Delores Armstead has not returned my call after 5 days. We must move forward. I had spoken with Keith Clinton. I thank God I found his number. I called him to get Rosina's number. As we spoke, we discussed the finances available to the school.

We must pass forward. I will need about $90,000. Ernell and I have about $100,000. God has the rest. I stay positive. $190,000 is A LOT. Rosina asked me if I had the money. I said, "Yes." I must believe and stay faithful. God will/has provide. Lord, thank You.

12/4/99 ~ 8:20 a.m.

Yesterday was a blessed day. Class 7 completed. All passed finals. Lord, thank You. Grace, the instructor, prayed and lectured, and prayed. We all prayed. She taught them a lesson. They were worthy, they could learn.

I do believe in the end, they could see the difference in their ability to succeed versus what Jolene had done.

I know that there are some who will never appreciate our efforts. But that's okay. I had told them if I could educate just one of them, I would be pleased. I am pleased. Jean Stevenson has been fantastic as an educator and a team player. She turned the program around. She is soft spoken, intelligent, and determined. She will make this program a success under her leadership.

We prayed before we separated, Grace, Alicia, Michael, Jean, and I. We were led by Grace. God is blessing us. The spirit of the school is wonderful. Wendy, Matthew, and Margie are shopping for the Christmas tree. Monday, the holiday begins at Four-D Success Academy. There is such peace at Four-D. Lord, my God, thank You.

I spoke with Charlie Seymour yesterday. He is under the weather. We won't say sick. Not Charlie.

He has been home since Tuesday. I can hear the pattern of his breathing. I have known for some time he had perched lip breathing. He is short-winded and tires easily. He tells me his balance is off. He has not fallen though. I tell him to take deep breaths and let it out slowly.

Charlie has been and continues to be my mentor. My selfishness for his survival is purely for me and others who love and appreciate him. It is for the hundreds of kids he has aided. He is truly my friend, someone I love, my mentor.

I pray to God for his full recovery. He is working on the Golf Course. Lord, let him complete it. I fear if he doesn't do it, no one will. No one has his desire to succeed. He is the driving force. God will allow him to walk again with steady feet. He will return to the streets to beat the path for the Golf Course. He will continue to fight for kids. Charlie is God's personal warrior for children. He is chosen. Lord, thank You.

12/4/99 ~ 11:01 p.m.

Call from Priscilla. 21 students in the VN Class, seven showed up for grad rehearsal. 21 students are graduating. That's the entire class! Lord, thank You. I pray they are all successful, pass their boards, and have a blessed life. I pray they all appreciate God's goodness.

Thank You, Lord.

12/9/99 ~ 7:05 a.m.

Ernell turned 50 on December 7th. Tahira took the family out to dinner. We met at the Claim Jumper and had a wonderful time. We were there from 6-9 p.m.

On the 7th, I also received a fax from Jean Templeman. She is requesting additional information and clarification to my response of the allegation. I have written the response. The attack of the accuser runs deep. Jean submitted the allegations to the Bureau for Private Post Secondary (PPS). I don't know when this will end.

Today, Creflo Dollar said faith develops potential, for you don't get in trouble and develop faith. You develop faith, so when trouble comes, you don't run. You stand. Lack of faith will cause you to panic and run. Faith will cause you to stand, knowing God is in control. Tears came and rolled down my face. I understand what he is saying. If I didn't have my faith, I would run, respond in panic, not have sight on the Lord. I am so sorrowful of the other actions. So many have suffered because of them.

I will stand on (in) my faith. God has brought me this far, He will take me further. Four-D Success Academy will not close. It will grow and expand beyond boundaries. My Lord knows the heart of everyone.

I pray He gives clear vision and interpretation to the reviewer of my response, that they can discern the truth from the lies.

Today, we are having a Holiday Luncheon for the student body and a door-decorating contest.

Thank You, Lord, for another day,

12/10/99 ~ 11:35 p.m.

We are blessed. I got the second response off to Jean Templeman. I pray this satisfies all her requests from me. Jean Stevenson has to respond to questions by Wednesday the 15th. We are set for the Board Meeting in February 2000.

Today, I attended the African-American Initiative at the SB County Medical Center. I started not to go. I was late – 8:30. I had a staff meeting at 9:30. But I thought, *There is someone I need to meet. I better go in.* Glad I did. It was good to be in the presence of other recognized professionals. After the meeting, I spoke with Bruce Stager, CEO S.B. Community Hospital. I solicited his assistance in obtaining equipment for training. I shared briefly my conversation with Dwight Martin. I gave him my business card. Hopefully, he will follow up and respond. I also spoke with Al Twine about Delores' lack of (non) response to my calls. He did follow up. She was out today, but he will call her on Monday. Delores is well-aware of my financial needs, yet she has not responded to multiple calls. I will follow up next week. Tomorrow is the school Graduation at SB Cal State University. Mayor Valles will be the commencement speaker. We are expecting a very good turnout. 27-30 students will participate. Lord, thank You.

I spoke with Greg today. New projections. We can afford the new site. I must, (God must) come up with 10% - ($198,000). It is there and I will see it.

Lord, be my sight. Guide me.

12/14/99 ~ 12:45 p.m.

Sitting in San Francisco Hyatt. I have spent the last 3 days listening to Financial Aid issues presented by CASFAA. I and

Stephen Byabashaija, Director of Finance and Operations, have obtained information to enhance operations. I am interested in Distance Learning. I have hired a person to develop the website.

I'm at home with Ernell and Aisha. Steve told me the "program" for the Christmas party is good. I was surprised at that information. I only expected a good social time, not a program. I have not planned an outfit so I may go shopping.

12/18/99 ~ 9:57 a.m.

The Holiday Party was very nice, well-organized, delicious food, and happy guests. Approximately 60 people attended. The music was great, dance contest, two women earning $50 each, door prizes – 20 given, happy times. Great music.

I am so proud of the school and staff. The spirit is so wonderful. Margie Harris was selected as employee of the year for 1999. I have turned to Business Bank of California for the loan. Union Bank and the County are not moving for me. I am totally disgusted. I hope to have an answer by the 1st week of 2000.

I received written notice from The Visiting Nurse Association Services Dept. I was accepted as a Board Member. I will use the position to assist the organization, assess services, policies and procedures, and staffing. I will promote The Academy and be a good representation. Life is good. The Nursing Consultant, Jean Templeman informed the DON we would be on the February agenda and have a class for February. We all are looking forward to the year.

God, thank You.

Linda L. Smith

12/22/99 ~ 11:42 p.m.

Today, Charlie informed me he was selected as one of ten in the nation for his humane services. What an honor to know him. He and his family will be flown to Washington in February 2000. There are no boundaries for him. He has truly been a positive influence for me.

Today, we had a potluck – a delicious spread as usual. We exchange gifts. The staff brought me a burgundy attaché-case. Total class. I must now live up to the position, a gift totally unexpected. I said the prayer for lunch. I gave thanks to the staff and to God for another year's end. My thoughts ran through my mind. I kept my tears to myself. I am unspeakably thankful.

Eugene Gonzales Jr., Vice President/SBA Manager for California Bank of San Bernardino, seems very positive. He received a tour, met staff, and discussed the plans for growth. I am so prayerful for a positive outcome.

At the end of the day, I was alone in the school. I stood at the back door to class 4. Stillness, I prayed. There I stood, eyes closed, left hand in contact with the door, fingers spread apart, I prayed repeatedly to God. Thanking Him for the year. I thanked God for the faith and for the challenges that improved our operations, deepened my faith, caused me to turn totally and only to God. I thanked God. We came to the end of a blessed year. I thanked God. His grace and His mercy has sustained us. His grace and His mercy will protect us. His grace and His mercy will move us forward.

God's grace is mine. I thank Him for Four-D Success Academy, Inc.

I journeyed home to my family. Peace is mine. The Lord is good. No matter what!

Happy Birthday, Jesus.

12/24/99 ~ 8:42 a.m.

It is the day before Christmas and all is well. Love filled my arms last night as my husband and I embraced. Tears flowed from my eyes as I uttered, "Ernell, I love you. I love you." He held me lightly and simply replied, "I know, I know." We are inseparable. We slip into sleep holding each other. Lord, thank You for Your grace and mercy.

12/25/99 ~ 12:05 a.m.

It's Christmas Day, Christ's Birthday. This evening, Ernell and I were guests of Cheryl and Roger Dublet. We and others feast on gumbo, sweet desserts, and conversation. I had not seen David, Thomas, or their wives and kids in over a year. We agreed we needed to spend more time together. I enjoyed myself. I had been emotionally isolated too long. It was good to be out.

Earlier, I stopped by Donna's for 2 hours. I had to see her before the end of the year. My old friend and I always have conversation of the positive, spiritual nature. I left her home with a smile.

I ran into Dorothy at Mel's Store. She suggested I have a summer get together potluck style this coming year. Not a bad thought. She told me to get out more. We must have lunch! This evening my kitchen had 2 cooks. Tahira was cooking greens and Aisha was making a cake for Jesus. I made four sweet potato pies. My home was filled with gospel, Christmas spirituals, laughter, conversation, and joy.

Lord, I thank You for so, so much.

Happy Birthday, Jesus.

12/25/99 ~ 9:15 a.m.

Merry Christmas. The girls are up at 7:30 a.m. with Ernell. I rose on command from Aisha at 8:00 a.m. It was time to open the gifts. I was instructed by Aisha to put on my robe. I always wear a robe to open the gifts. Gathered in the living room, I sat with the others. Aisha reminded me it was my job to pass the gifts out. *Rise and get busy.* I handed Tahira a gift. Aisha, Ernell, silence, expressed looks, smiles, and thank you's for the sweaters and pants. Then Aisha opens a gift from Tahira. Her eyes widen. Her smile is even bigger. I want to know what it is. Diamond earrings. I can see them from across the room. Tahira is a big hit with her sister. More exchanges. Tahira received sweaters, tops, and money to aid in the backyard of her home. Ernell received tennis shoes, pants, shirts, sweaters, and dress shoes. I got under garments, a night gown, a purse, and a RENEWED love vow from my husband. I open a lovely gift box; inside of it was a small black velvet box. *Hope to find a necklace.* I thought. I opened it. Silent screams, repeatedly from my mouth.

No sounds from me as I held the long-awaited wide banded marquee diamond ring. It is beautiful. I cried and cried. Later as I sat next to Tahira, I told Ernell he was supposed to ask me to marry him.

He came over and asked me to take off the ring. I gave it to him.

In the presence of our children, he knelt. With the ring in his hand, he placed the diamond on my wedding finger saying these words, *"I renew my love for you for the next 25 years."* We kissed and hugged.

The girls watched in silence. Our moment of love, of exchange, our joy. Our family. We are so blessed.

Now we prepare to visit family for more joy, blessings, hugs, tears, and laughter.

Merry Christmas, Jesus.

12/25/99 ~ 11:31 p.m.

We had a wonderfully blessed day. We first visited Momma and the twins. Donnie was over. We passed out the gifts, talked, and ate. Momma received a 2-piece pant set. The top was silver and black, the pants black. The twins received velour tops. Anwar got red and green for Jaise. After a two-hour stop, we continued to Mom's house for more gifts, talking, and eating. By 3:00 p.m., we had exchanged gifts. I, of course, displayed my ring with a big smile. It is quite impressive in the setting. We talked with Bunty about the bedroom sit and couch. She graciously accepted both. She said the blessings just keep coming. I was concerned she would think we were giving handouts. But not the case – it is best to give to the family in need. Bunty appreciated God's gift.

Ernell will deliver everything to her, Tahira's couch set and our set. It is a wonderful day. We arrived home by 8:00 p.m. Tahira is working tonight.

My husband loves me unconditionally. When we were in the trial/tribulation of our marriage 3 years ago, I did not think he would accept me/love me enough to keep us together. When we decided to stay married, I still thought his love was conditional. I began to gain weight. I had thoughts of gaining weight up to 200 lbs. Well, I weigh between 190-200 lbs. Today, he vowed his love for another 25 years. His love for me is unconditional. Tonight, I decided to lose the weight I have gained. I will control my intake, drink 8-10 glasses of water daily, take care of myself, live for my family and me. Ernell once told me I could control my business and work hard. I can lose weight if I choose to. I choose to. I choose to lose the weight.

Aisha baked a cake for Jesus' Birthday. We gathered around the table at Momma Vivian and sung Happy Birthday to Jesus. Momma Vivian says Aisha is destined for great things. She just knows it. I don't doubt it. Happy Birthday, Jesus! I will lose the excess weight.

12/28/99 ~ 7:57 a.m.

Yesterday, I toured the new site with Stephen, Jean, and Kaye. They had great ideas to minimize the demolition of the building for TI's. We are all excited about the future of the Academy. These recommendations cut the cost from $385,000 to about $290,000. I spoke with Eugene from Business Bank. They are willing to move forward if I obtain a signed statement that the County will retain the clinic. I placed a call to Al Twine and the County Realtor Office; both are out until 1/3/2000. I will call Supervisor Eaves today to seek assistance. I informed Ernell of the progress. He is confident in his words, "You'll get the loan." I asked if he was concerned in any way about becoming owner. He said, "No," and kept eating peanuts.

I spent time yesterday talking to Michael from Minolta. He mentioned "difficulties this year." I told him those challenges will only make his faith stronger. I look at challenges as opportunities to grow spiritually, to believe in God. My roots deepen into the soil of faith.

It is always a blessing to witness to another.

Thank You, Lord.

Love Your Child, Linda

Jean Templeman called Jean Stevenson today. She informed Jean the Nursing Program would receive a violation regarding the clinical hours. She would not say if her recommendation was in favor of the school. Left weary and uneasy, Jean and I sat in silence for a while. We then say we just have to pray through this, adjust, and keep going. We thought about contacting the President, C. Bennet or Ann Shuman Super. But after some time, we realized we should not go over Jean's head. Greg Sheets called, his interpretation of the Regulations of the Department of Education requires us to raise 25% of the received SEOG funds awarded. We need $41,875. The financial audit would reflect a liability on our statement. Neither the Academy nor I have $41,000 to return to the Department of Education. We must wait until Monday to contact the department. No, I will call tomorrow. A student, C. Turner, reported Mr. Cann as being rude, cussing, creating a confrontation with her, and disrespecting a patient. I will investigate these charges. Mr. Cann denies these charges. By the end of the day, I was heavy-hearted. I called Charlie.

Charlie talked to me about God. Delete negative from my vocabulary. God has it marked out. My faith must sustain above all. I read Sadiq's letters of encouragement, his words to keep faithful to God. All is well. I watched the People's Choice Awards. Someone said, "Quitting is not an option." No, quitting is not an option for me. I sat down and drafted a letter to Mr. Earvin "Magic" Johnson. I seek his support to aid the school with repayment. I have prayed, cried, and prayed. My pain is in knowing that there are those who are against us. All that I try to do to help others. They would hurt those I am trying to help. How could they? I cry with a sad heart, a heart full of sorrow. God hears my words of sadness. He will answer.

Lord, thank You. My covenant is with You, not the world. Thank You.

Your Child, Linda

12/30/99 ~ 7:08 a.m.

I awakened at 3:20 a.m. with prayer upon my lips. I sought Jesus in my sleep. I was praying for the school. I asked for wisdom, guidance, insight. I prayed for the students. I prayed for forgiveness of my enemies, those who sought to destroy. As I prayed the prayer for forgiveness, I knew the Lord had transformed me. I had moved beyond my pain into the realm of forgiving. My heart was light, my mind clean, my thoughts focused. I know my prayers were received.

As I lay in the early morning night, I began to think of many things. I reached for the pen and pad on the nightstand. I began to write line after line in the dark. My thoughts flowed freely, my hand steady as I had seen all that was to be done. I visualized the workstation of the new site, who should go where, best positioning, policy/procedures from departments, receptionist duties, contracts, follow-up.

I thanked the Lord for all. Returning the pad and pen to the nightstand, I dozed for another hour or so. "Ask anything in My name and believe." I believe.

12/30/99 ~ 11:22 p.m.

I arrived at work by 8:33 a.m. into an empty parking lot. No students, no staff, no visitors. Quiet, peaceful. I sat in my chair and said a silent prayer. I got busy. Writing memos, letters, telephone calls to Washington trying to reach Alice Payne, in Virginia to talk with Carol Moneymaker, calls to Jean. S, Stephen, Greg Sheets, and Ernell.

Greg informed me we may have to pay $38,000 back to the Department of Education if we don't receive the waiver. Stephen thinks we can receive a waiver. I will reach Alice on Monday.

I shared with Ernell the latest with Jean Templeman, the Department of Education, and my concerns he would not want to move forward with the building. Ernell said it would work out. I began to cry. My husband said okay. I told him I needed his support. I thanked him and returned to work.

I will seek another CPA per Greg's request. He is unable to keep up with the CPA duties with his Tax business and consulting. I was calm. Life changes. I called Shawn Washington CPA for his resume.

Home at 6:30 p.m. A full, productive day came to an end. I'm now resting in my husband's arms at 12 midnight.

Lord, thank You for a good day.

1/1/2000

A new century began with my family joined in a circle holding hands. I said a silent prayer of thanks to God. My family, we are where we should be—together.

As I watched the activity around the world, I was struck psychologically by Maya Angelou's words. She spoke at the Lincoln Memorial Site. She spoke of compassion, kindness, and forgiveness. I thought of my/Four-D Success plight and the possible financial impact if we must return $41,000 back to the Department of

Education. I thought of those who were against the Academy. I realized in the depth of my soul I traveled a path, which I do not know where it leads, but I know I must stay on it. The contractor who laid the path is God. There are no accidents on His roads. An unexplainable calmness fills me, no fear. Peace, all is well.

For my family is with me. For that, I give all praises to God. Lord, thank You.

Your Child, Linda

1/1/2000 ~ 1:54 p.m.

Awakened at 8:00 a.m. to the ringing sounds resonating in my ears. The telephone had a caller. Sadiq's voice said, "Good morning. Girl, did I wake you up?" I sleepily said no, I was just dozing and resting. We talked for a few minutes. He gave me something to think about – marriage to a young lady. We will have further discussions on this. He informed me Donnie is back living with Momma. His "lady" left him for lack of support. She took her five kids and left.

Momma will never acknowledge Donnie's faults. But he is her child and she is his mother. Momma has been there for all of us.

I spoke with Stephen about the waiver issue. Had he given Greg the impression I knew of the waiver option and elected not to apply for it? Stephen reminded me he had come to my office in September 1999. I had just finished meeting with Jolene. (I had terminated her.) As he spoke to me about the FISAP Report and the waiver, I got up and walked out of the office. I was gone for a while. When I returned, I stayed in my office. That was the day I walked out to sing myself through all the pain. I walked and cried and sang *Lead me, Guide me*. I sang until the pain was gone. Alone, walking, I prayed. God is with me. I was so hurt, full of sorrow and grief. No anger. Disappointed. Why would anyone want to harm the school and the students? There was so much I didn't understand. I cried, and I prayed.

I remember that day. I couldn't hear a word Stephen was saying. I was too full. Monday, he and I will review the original application, contact Alice Payne, and do what is right for the Academy.

Ernell has gone snow skiing. Aisha is at the mall. I am home, in my element. I like being home alone to think, do a little, and enjoy my life.

Lord, thank You.

Oh yeah, I called Momma Julie for the New Year and a good laugh. I told her she lived into the next century. She didn't die. As usual, she said, "Yeah I am here, but I am not doing too well." Her famous line. But she is here at the age of 90. Momma Julie, I do love you.

1/2/2000 ~ 11:05 p.m.

A spirit filled day. While driving to Church, the spirit of God filled me. I praised Him while driving. Tears of joy filled my eyes.

It is so wonderful to feel His presence. At Church during the altar call, I gave Aisha my things – purse, Bible – and walked forward. The minister gave a powerful prayer to the congregation. I lifted my hands to God, open to receive His many blessings. I prayed for my mother, in-laws, family, friends, the school, students, and approval from the board. I prayed for my soul to forgive those who desire to do harm. I prayed to God to heal my heart. No anger. I forgive those who have anger in their hearts against the school and me. I prayed for their salvation. I prayed that they are able to forgive. Tears flowed through the service, God's presence comforted me, my heart, my soul, my spirit lifted to God, my provider. The forgiver above all. I was asked to return to the Choir by the section director. I will.

The year is blessed. We are in God's hands. I walk a path lit by God. I don't know where it will lead. But I will stay on it. I will follow the path lit by the light. Thank You, Lord.

A Grateful Linda

1/5/2000 ~ 11:50 p.m.

I received a "revised" financial statement from Greg, CPA. The adjustments reduced the net income from $49,000 to $47,000. The SEOG grants were not matched by 25% and the PELL was over-awarded. Therefore, the school must deduct the difference from the bottom line. I spoke with Alice Payne from the Department of Education. She explained the process and gave me a name referred on policy of the Department of Ed. We received the written responses from Jean Templeman, Consultant. Five of the six allegations were found "insufficient evident." The school was found in violation of not meeting the attendance requirements for clinical training. Jean identified four Wednesdays not documented. Jean Stevenson and Priscilla are receiving attendance rosters on all grades in class 7. Our goal is to identify shortages in clinical hours, and inform the students and set makeup days during the next two weeks.

We do not know Jean Templeman's recommendation to the Board. I make contact with Trudy Smith with the Real Estate Department for San Bernardino County. Trudy sounds helpful on providing a letter of intent. Once received, I will submit it to Eugene at Business Bank of California.

I informed Ernell of the finances and loan process. It is very important that he be fully aware of the current situation of the school.

He feels comfortable. He gave his consent to move forward.

I met the finance team. Stephen, Juanita, and Pat discuss the process of distribution of the actual available operating dollars over the next six months.

Student loans, CNA's, it's 12:30 a.m. 1-6-2000. Stay focused, keep believing. Yesterday a minister said, "When you are faced with trouble, turn to God." I stand before God in spirit and truth. I will press on in faith. All of the problems strengthen the school. We pursue that which is good, dismissing the bad. Prayer will keep the school going. It is the cement to our foundation. Prayer keeps me. Goodnight, my Lord.

1/7/2000 ~ 10:55 p.m.

Jean S. and Priscilla B. have been reviewing each student's attendance. Analysis will determine how many hours each student must make up to have 960 clinical hours. The students in class 9 and 10 were notified of the Nurse Consultant's decision. Students in class 7 are being contacted by Jean Stevenson. Eugene Gonzalez, VP of SBA with Business Bank of California, said we and another will tour the 1020 Washington Building on Monday p.m. I will need to contact Supervisor Eave's office for a letter of support. The letter the bank received from the County Real Estate office was not "strong" enough. I am confident that I will get the letter.

Tomorrow is my mother's Birthday. Eula Mae Russ will be 75 years old/young. I called to take her out to breakfast. She turned me down.

She has things to do – take the boys to class, prepare her dinner! That's why she declined my invitation to the concert *"Woman Thou Art Loose."* She is planning her annual Birthday Dinner Party for the Usher Board. I will try to locate her and present my gifts!

I received a position lecture-information session with Charlie. How to get the customer format for the non-profit company, Alumni, adopt-a-school – Colton High. He has so much inside, he tires me. But I listen. Charlie has Four-D Success Academy at heart. I thank God for him, his advice, and his guidance. My personal mentor.

1/9/2000 ~ 11:25 p.m.

Yesterday was Momma's 75th Birthday. I delivered a dozen red roses to the house. She was out, as usual. I called her at 6:00 p.m. She was home, but I was interrupting her process. She was preparing for her guests. A quick hello, I love you, and goodbye. She informed me Donnie was taking her to dinner after Church. In other words, don't look for me tomorrow. God, keep her in good health and positive spirits.

Ernell, Tahira, Aisha, and I went to see "Women Thou Art Loose," a play by T.D. Jakes. We all enjoyed each other. It was wonderful having my family together. Dinner was on Tahira – Carl's Jr. Then we went home. Today at Church, Pastor Chuck taught from Joshua 7:1-6. He spoke on sin. Sin of one can affect the whole. If the whole allows the sin (to exist), we put ourselves in situations which allow sin. Even our thoughts can sin. Protect our actions and thoughts from sin. Prayer is not a substitute for repentance. As I listened, I thought of my sins. My prayer for forgiveness, for redemption, my repentance. God forgave.

Aisha came into my room and asked if I recalled last Sunday's message from Joshua 6, the march around Jericho. How God had given the instruction to walk seven times around the walls of Jericho for six days and on the seventh day, to shout victory.

She asked if I had been praying for the building. Had I gone to the building to pray? I had. She then instructed me to walk, as the Israelites did, around the building, and pray. So when I get it, I can shout! I will shout unto the Lord.

I asked Robert Rochelle to pray with me. I felt the need to have a prayer warrior. He has always supported the school. Robert submitted a prayer to the Lord to bless the school, to remove the stumbling blocks, to heal the hearts of the prosecutors. No weapon shall form against the school shall prosper. "Greater is He that is within me then he that is in the world." The tears flowed. God takes care of all. The flow of tears released my sorrow and pain. I don't doubt God. God has been my Rock. My sorrow is for those that are in the world.

Tomorrow, I will rise, call Joe for a tour of the building at 1:00, and call Al Twine. I will get the letter from Supervisor Eaves for the building.

Goodnight, Lord.

1/12/2000 ~ 11:30 p.m.

I received the 2nd letter from the San Bernardino County Real Estate Department. It was more positive than the 1st letter. It was faxed to Eugene. He and I spoke about the expected outcome. I stressed to him I didn't want the Board to speak with the CPA, Operations, or my assistant. I had to speak for the school's financials. I did not need anyone casting doubt on this opportunity. He and I have something to gain. Eugene informed me the Board would not call anyone. He was ready to proceed. Jim, the VP of Credit, said they would make it work. The school's finances and Ernell's income was adequate to cover the mortgage = $14,000/month. The Board will meet at 8:30 a.m. I am to call his cell phone at 10:00 a.m. I know God has laid this plan.

I called and spoke with Ann Shuman, VN Supervisor, regarding the requirements of Jean Templeman. I expressed my concern of possible legal actions against the school if we were forced to have students return to make up 4 days after they were issued certificates of completion. I expressed the position of the Academy regarding the VN regulations. The school had followed the instructional plan. The regulations do not require perfect attendance; the student must show clinical competency. Betty Davenport never reported any inadequacy of students, she never reported cancelling class, and I don't know what assignment, if any, she gave the students. The students are shocked at her behavior. Betty is not trustworthy. The alleged absence occurred in April/May. The report was not submitted to the Board until November, six months later. The Academy has never received the organized attendance roster. I expressed the fact that Betty had befriended a student by moving her out of her home from the husband to a relative's home. Ann said she would speak with Jean. I also informed Ann that I had rescinded my request to have a December class after speaking with Jean T. We had agreed Jean S. was new and we needed to focus on the current population. I did as I had indicated to the Board. I dismissed students who were inadequate in performance and attendance. I took the financial loss, expecting not to hold a class for 7-8 months. Financially, it would devastate the school. I requested her consideration. I don't believe Ann was fully aware of Jean T.'s actions, the 'nonexistent' conversation between Jean and I. I do believe we will have the February start date. Four-D Success Academy will have the opportunity to bless a whole new group of students, have a positive spiritual effect, provide knowledge, and change lives.

In three hours, Ernell will spring from bed, call Aisha and I to rise, dress, and prepare for the airport departure at 4:00 a.m. We are going to Vancouver, Canada, for the Annual Ski Trip. We will have a wonderful safe trip. Tahira elected not to go. She started with the State (Prison) and she has money to make.

1/13/2000 ~ 11:25 a.m.

Here we are in Vancouver, Canada, the Brotherhood of Skiers. Ernell, Aisha, and I safely arrived with all others. I am watching the hands on the watch. We landed 10 minutes ahead of schedule (It was 10:20 a.m.), gathered our luggage, and checked through customs. I began to look for a telephone. It's 11:00 a.m. Using the American Express card, I dialed Eugene Gonzales's cell phone number. He picked up on the second ring. "Eugene, this is Linda." He sounded calm, his voice gave no excitement. I thought, *Oh my,* but asked, "How did it go?"

He responded calmly, "It was approved." There are some contingencies, which we discussed. The plans, contractor's letter, these are needed as soon as possible to help the escrow value. Excitement shot through me. My God, approved for $1,792,000. My God, He works miracles. I felt excitement run through my body. My smile grew wide, all teeth showing. I let out a happy shout. A man next to me thought I was happy to be in Canada. "No, not that. This is better,"

I responded. I hung up the telephone and searched the crowd. I was frantically looking for Ernell and Aisha. The look on my face and my smile would tell them the good news. I spotted Aisha first across the room. I gave her a thumbs-up. Ernell walked up and I said, "We got it!"

Ernell, being himself, said calmly, "I told you that you would get it." Now we come up with the money. God's plan and only I know how He worked it. Lord, thank You. Now Jean will hear from the Nursing Board. The results are in our favor. God is in control.

The foundation. God established the foundation. It's solid, built on a rock.

Lord, thank You. Linda, Ernell, and Four-D

1/13/2000 ~ 11:20 p.m.

Upon returning to the Wildwood Lodge at 2:30, I had an urgent call from Wendy. My first thought was that I couldn't leave for 12 hours. What could it be? The word "urgent" shook me. I called to retrieve the message. A reporter from the SB Press Enterprise wanted to interview me for an article. It would appear in tomorrow's paper. I called the reporter, Joann, who was interviewing African-American Business Owners. She was seeking info on how I got started, hurdles faced, financial resources, student population, distance they've come. I shared much but I told her I was working on something. I wanted her to write a story. She said okay. Believe me, I will call her in 30 days. She will fax a copy of the article to the office tomorrow. I stressed to her that my faith keeps going.

At 4:30 I received another call. The bank wanted to do the appraisal tomorrow. I gave Jay at the bank Mike's office number. I then called

Mike and left a message to give them Joe's number. Okaying access to the building.

Ann Shuman did not call Jean Stevenson today. Jean Templeman apparently did not come in.

We have had a pleasant time thus far here. The weather is cold between -13 and 30 degrees. Light snow falling. The trees are covered with snow, the mountains the same. The environment looks like a postcard.

Well, tomorrow I will ski. I don't have a choice. Many have asked the same question. "Well Linda, are you hitting the slopes tomorrow?" I smile, "More than likely. After all, Ernell has purchased all of the gear I need."

This has been a full day.

Lord, thank You.

1/14/2000

I spoke with Jean Stevenson, DON. She had a conference call with Jean Templeman and Ann Shuman. They will recommend the Board not approve class for February 4th. I called Jean T. and requested a start of 15 students. She conferred with Ann and another. They will not rescind the denial recommendation. With a heavy heart and silent tears running down my face, I became numb. Yesterday was a grand feeling of success. Interviews, approval for the loan to purchase a building, and now this. The financial impact and negative publicity will be heavy. I will discuss the next step with Ernell. On Tuesday, I will meet with Jean S. and Stephen B. I will talk with Mike Ballard and with Richard Nevins, Attorney.

We must look at the financial strategy to survive. Staff cuts, advertisement cuts in the press and Sun Telegram. The loan requested a lease with an option to purchase? What will the rent be on 20 square feet? What is the financial impact on the students who must finish the program? Will they return back into the current module? My Lord, guide us through this valley. Survival will make us better.

1/15/2000 ~ 12:30 a.m.

Bewildered, I sat in the chair for several hours. My mind confused, tormented. Aisha realized my state of mind. I looked up and she was combing my hair. Holding my hand, she began to stroke gently, parting the strands. Aisha rolled my hair as I sat in the chair, staring blindly at the T.V. When she finished, she sent me to bed.

Entering the shower, my heart ached with pain. The bellow of my bowel is so empty. Tears could not come forth. Sadness, sorrow, unspeakable anguish flooded me. As the millions of water droplets sprung from the shower, I thought of them as my tears. If I could cry, yes, my tears would flow as the droplets from the shower.

I thought of the meanness of the others. Satan never stops planning against Jesus' children. They hurt the students to hurt the school, to hurt me. Why not attack me and leave the students to succeed in life? I tried to save them, to pray with them, to convince them the instructor meant them no good. Blindsided, they walked and talked themselves into the trap.

I was sitting in my room when Aisha came in to talk. I had reconsidered what wonderful blessing God would give me out of this. I know He will give me a testimony. Aisha and I talked. I explained the repercussions of the Nursing Board actions, the loss of funds, the building, students, the effect on the school's reputation. She told me to sit still and let God do! God needed me to be still. Tomorrow, be quiet for Jesus. No planning, no looking at options, no thinking the worst. Let God be God. Then my child said, "Let's pray." My child said a powerful prayer to God on the school and my behalf. The tears of joy flowed. My blessing was experiencing my child's love for Christ, her belief and the expression of love for me. Her prayer expressed my knowledge, my love, and my long hours and dedication to the school and the school. I cried joyful tears. I heard my child pray.

God has a plan and I have a testimony. I will be still and listen to God. Aisha, thank you. The word of God says the children will speak the truth.

My Heavenly Father, thank You for my child.

1/15/2000 ~ 11:37 a.m.

Here in this quiet room, I make notes of what to do. I pray to God for guidance. I call Jean S. We discuss options. I call Charlie; he reminds me always there is no power that can separate me from God. My best competition is my sales person. "God is God and truth. Sing *Amazing Grace*. It will work out." I always call Charlie for I know he will only speak of God's power and truth. No tears. No negative energy. Only God's will and truth. I should be enjoying myself. I will get dressed and go join Ernell and Aisha.

1/15/2000 ~ 11:47 p.m.

Well, the end of the day. I sat here earlier in dismay. After talking with Charlie, I got dressed to venture to the Mountain Top to have lunch with Ernell and Aisha. I sang as I went. By 3:30, I was heading back to the room. Mike Ballard had called. I returned the call. I informed him of the Nursing Consultant decision, the financial impact. He and I will talk next week of a strategy to keep the deal. Mike and I have spent much time on trying to close a deal. Within 24 hours, jubilation succumbed to a state of sorrow. Ernell wants me to pursue the matter with the past employee and Cherry with an attorney. The financial loss is a minimum of $550,000+.

I listened to spirituals, hummed *Amazing Grace*. Sang my way through it. The evening has come to an end. I had dinner with Ernell and Aisha. I miss Tahira, but she is working and didn't want to take the time off. Tomorrow is a new day to receive God's blessing.

Goodnight, Lord.

1/16/2000 ~ 12:35 p.m.

Everyone is up (the skiers) at 6:00 a.m. They headed out at 7:00 a.m. for the early morning snow. I lay in bed thinking of God. I needed quiet time. They left, and I rose and changed the batteries in the disc player.

I returned to bed and listened to Gospel and prayed until 10:30, songs of God's love, protection, and guidance. I listened and became calm in spirit. God cares, He loves, He protects. I had a talk with God, over and over. The words penetrated my mind, I listened, I prayed, I sang. I prayed to my Lord for peace, protection, guidance. He knows the outcome. I asked for guidance to stay on the narrow path of righteousness. I prayed for consolation of staff to be of one mind to pursue excellence to aid the students. I prayed He bind up the enemy(s) and cast them out. I prayed that whatever I pursue in the legal rim, I do it without malice.

The song of God's love and omnipresence gives me comfort. I know that I am in the protection of God. Four-D Success has a purpose. God intended it to be. It will continue.

I called Charlie to thank him for his support and words of God's protection and love. He told me to make lemonade out of lemons. I thought of what to do – a mentor. I was interviewed on Friday. The article was due to come out on Saturday. He said he would pick it up. I thought of contacting Ed Maul or Joanne Foster to write an article on the school. The problems make lemonade. Contact Mike Ballard, set up a home saving plan for students to purchase home with 6-10 months post grad. Contact the Ford dealership – set up a program for students to purchase cars. Start the Spanish conversation class. Make lemonade out of lemons.

I sit here at Wildwood room 313. The blinds are vertically open. Snow lightly falling, the trees are heavily covered with pure white bright snow, the treetop extending into the sky. Unable to distinguish the boundary of the sky from the tip of the pine trees, I look at the peace of God and know all is well with the Lord. My breathing at ease, no torment inside. I am growing to God, to know of His protection. The peace is knowing Him.

God is good. I am his child. Lord, thank You.

1/17/2000 ~ 11:25 p.m.

State Holiday – Dr. Martin Luther King Jr. He too had a dream, a vision. He followed God's path for him. I had a dream, a vision. I follow God's path for me. Tomorrow, I will arrive at work with goodwill and cheer. I will continue to ask God, "What do I do now, what do I do next?" I ask Him to guide my path, protect the students, the school and all it stands for.

On the flight home from Canada, I looked out of the window. Above the clouds, I always feel God's presence. As far as I can see, it is endless. His creation. Surely He sees me. He knows my heart, my needs. I have faith and love in God. I have solemn peace. I closed my eyes and prayed to my Heavenly Father! I fell asleep.

Now, home in bed. I am blessed. My husband, child, and I arrived home without injury.

Lord, my Lord, lead me. Guide me along the way.

Your Child, Linda

1/21/2000 ~ 10:21 p.m.

The week has come to an end. Friday night is here. It has been a long week – productive. Ernell and I signed the loan paper – forwarded to Mike. I am requesting Escrow to end April 17, 2000. This will allow a start in April, time to generate more money, time for the seller to relocate the tenant and reduce the property line. The plans must be drawn. Otis must place written bids.

I have to talk with Linda Stratton about the current leases. We must be out June 7, 2000 or obtain an extension.

Jean and Priscilla are working on the preparation for the Nurse Consultant's visit. We are moving items, setting up better skill labs, etc. Stephen and I are looking at the financial status. Monday, I will present a proposal to the staff to take 1 day less per pay period to avoid a financial shortfall, as well as a bonus system.

I spoke with Walter Jr. about a Ground Training Aeronautics School. I will write a grant for funding. I expect it to be ready in 30-45 days.

Parent Conference with Jaise and Anwar's teacher. They are doing okay. They need to focus on math and reading. I took them to dinner and we talked about how they are children of God. As long as they know that, nothing should interfere with their focus. Stay in school to prepare for College. No fighting, no poor language, etc. Hugs, kisses, and words of love given.

I feel peaceful, energized. We will forge ahead. As I wrote today, challenges create better character. Challenges increase the spiritual faith in God.

With God, all things are possible. Lord, thank You for making me better.

1/24/2000

Yesterday was a day of spiritual growth for me. I rose, turned on the T.V. to my Sunday T.V. sermons. Pastor Stanley was teaching on "God's Way to Success." Learning lessons from hardship, stay focused on the goals. I ordered the tape and book. Another minister spoke on Romans 12:17-21. It tells of forgiving and letting God be God. Do not seek revenge. Stay focused. At the NCNW Area meeting, a presenter read Scripture. It continued to aid in confirmation of the decision I had made. I called my attorney Richard Nevins, left a message. I will not pursue the legal actions against the 3 nurses. I will let God be God. He knows what they did was wrong. He will guide our path.

Lord, thank You.

1/26/2000 ~ 11:49 p.m.

The $35,000 was submitted to Business Bank of California to cover the appraised fee. We are moving forward. More papers signed and submitted. Tomorrow, I will make rounds of the building with a planner and a computer technologist.

I attended my first Board Meeting with the Visiting Nurse Association Support Services, Inc. I received a warm welcome, participated in discussion, made inquires, and signed up for the Business Laws Committee and the Finance and Budget Committee. This will be a very positive Business/Professional venture for me, and Sadiq's book, finally, is finished. Under distress, I only ordered 100 for print. I was desperate to deliver the order to the school district. I just could not think clearly. I was under so much pressure. Now I must work through a process to access funds to market the book. I know I am sitting on a mint, as Tammy Monroe would put it.

I presented a letter to the staff regarding donation of 1 day of pay per pay period. The response was excellent. God will guide our path. I submitted final papers to B of A for a line of Credit for $100,000. I pray/meditate daily to stay in positive spirits. The finances are tight, productive, marginal. Wendy attended an Advertisement Workshop. She returned fired up. Ideas to promote First Aid and Cont. Ed Classes.

We are preparing the VN visit. Tomorrow will be a blessed-another-day. Goodnight, Lord.

1/31/2000 ~ 7:47 a.m.

Glory, glory, glory, glory. God's glory is with me. Lord, thank You for this day.

1/31/2000 ~ 10:15 p.m.

My day started peaceful and it ends peaceful. I arrived to work with joy in my heart. While driving to work, I sang a spiritual, which I had leaned on as a child. We Are Soldiers. In God's army; lead me, guide me; Glory, Glory, Grace. I sang down the freeway, praising the Lord. Around 9:20 a.m. I received a call from Yolanda. I had met her in person on Thursday, the week before. A space planner. She is doing the layout for the new building. I thought she was calling about the building, but she immediately began to witness about God's blessing. Her personal situation with her husband, kids, and business ventures. As she praised God for carrying her through, she began to witness to me to stay focused, stay on path, and anoint myself with oil from head to toe. Anoint my feet to walk in the right path. She told me God had given me the vision and He had the provision. Praise in song, sit still and let God be God. His message was coming through her. She was a vessel sent by God. I began to praise the Lord, my feet separated from the floor. Tears filled my eyes and traveled down my cheeks. She blessed me. We never talked about the building. We agreed to take the time to praise God. Talk on the building would come later. I went to Riverside to meet with Holly. We discussed the Academy providing "training" of all programs, a presentation in May, a positive meeting.

Stephen received the tentative notice from the Department of Education. We were approved for $43,000 for the Work Study Program and $124,000 for the SEOG. That's $4,000 more. He anticipated they might increase it once the adjusted application is reviewed.

Betty Thomas informed me she was going on a fast from 12 midnight to 8:00 p.m. to pray for the school. I agreed with her. My purpose to fast and pray till 8:00. Lord, thank You. Yolanda's message included having a prayer partner to keep lifting up. Lord, thank You.

2/2/2000 ~ 11:37 p.m.

Today, I signed the Riverside contract for the VN and CNA Program. I had not visited the Riverside Office in over two years. We had not received a referral in more than 8 months. Are the tables turning following my meeting with Holly? I spoke with the landlord of the Cooley Lease. I requested to extend the lease month by month. I shall get an answer in a week. Yolanda will locate the building plans of the Washington building. I stay focused, keeping my spirit intact with the Lord. I seek wisdom and peace. God is guiding my path. Lord, what will happen on Friday? Let Four-D Success Academy have favor with the VN Board. My Lord, keep us all together. Your will always. Your path. I walk in faith.

2/3/2000

Today, I met Sharie Bercar, Assistant to the City of San Bernardino Reading Program. I introduced the book authored by Sadiq. Sharie was open to making the book *Traditional African-American Women Who Have Made a Difference in Life,* accessible to elementary students. She provided reference for contact presentations. I will need 200 more books for advertisement. I am excited about all the possibilities.

At the Black Health Initiative, I met a gentleman named Jim. We discussed the Jamal Project. He and I will meet to discuss his assistance in steering the proposal and directing it to the "right" person in Washington for funding.

Tomorrow, Jean Stevenson and I go to San Diego. We are on the agenda for the Board approval to start a class on February 7th. I believe God will provide a positive outcome. The truth does not pardon

102

error, but wipes it away in the most effective manner. We will be freed by the truth and God's love.

Lord, we are always under the umbrella of Your wings and we stand on the foundation of Your words. Ask and it shall be given. Believe in Him.

Goodnight, Lord.

2/4/2000

Well, heart at ease, I listened to the Nurse Supervisor read the Consultants report on the Academy. The crowd reacted to gushing sounds. Jean and I held our head high. The end results: Denial, no start on Monday. I sat and thought, *Okay Lord, there is a testimony here. We are not defeated*. I spoke with the staff. I stress positivity, focus, and the immediate plan to move forward. The discussion was upbeat, open, and supportive. We will strategize a plan of action. I informed Ernell of the outcome. He is supportive. We will talk on how to fund the building.

Lord, thank You for the peace. My faith lifts me up.

II Chronicles 20:25

The enemy will come to war with all the jewels. God will position Four-D Success Academy to gain victory.

Priscilla and I participated in the San Bernardino Black History Parade. She is a character, laughing, waving, and saying "hello" and "hola" to the Hispanics. We held our heads high and smiled wide. We are proud of who we are and we know where we are going. God is our protector.

We attended the Black Culture Dinner. I was asked by Frank Stallworth for my business card. During the announcements of guests, I was acknowledged. My work is recognized by the community members.

Ernell and I talked about the building. We have about $80,000. We need $100,000 more by April 17, 2000. Lord, I am believing in You for $100,000. Through God, all things are possible. Thank You, Jesus.

2/7/2000 ~ 10:47 p.m.

What a blessed day! Focus on prayer, staff members fasting, and gospel in room. Calling on God. The students arrived for class 12. Twenty-six ladies came. The 6 from the RN JTPA were waiting on the final approval from their case managers.

Jean and I entered into the room. I prayed that God would control the words I spoke and the thoughts I thought. I began.

I let the words flow from me, from my heart. Silence in the room. No angry facial expressions. I explained diplomatically the board's decision not to allow a class to start, what we wanted to do to prepare them for an April 17th start. We presented a preparatory outline covering study habits, accountability, and responsibility. Math, Analogy, and Philosophy. They listened to the desires of the program to make them a success. They were tested, filled out a questionnaire, and wrote an essay. Totally cooperative. We prayed. I gave a brief history of the school and my role, the prayer process, and why we pray. No objections.

They left at 12:00 noon, vowing to return on 3/1/2000 for class. Tomorrow, the consultant will come. The house is filled with God. Goodnight.

2/9/2000 ~ 10:30 p.m.

Well, Jean Templeman and Ann Sherman ended their two-day assessment. I am grateful Ann was present. She eased the blows from Jean. Jean wanted to issue a violation for not having a current geriatric book in the library. <u>One</u> book. Jean Stevenson informed the pair that each student's book had an excellent section on gerontology. Ann Sherman dismissed the violation. Jean did stick us with a violation. One in six hospitals – objections not posted. I did question the quantitative ratio. How serious is it to warrant a violation? Jean S. has much to do to submit a request to be on the April agenda. Both ladies state they see a positive change. We are in the right direction. We forge ahead.

I attended the graduation for the students of Adopt-A-Bike/Computer. Twenty-seven children/young adults graduated. The twins Anwar and Jaise were among them.

Lord, I am tired/sleepy.

2/10/2000 ~ 10:30 p.m.

What is God's plan for the Academy? As I see the financial status of the school, I realize the need to obtain revenue. The denial to start a class had a negative impact of $500,000. That was the intent. I question the activity of the consultant. She is not as friendly and helpful as she projects. She writes negative reports such as, "The school library is inadequate in resource materials." When actually, only one book was needed to address the Geriatric Study. There are over 100 videos and numerous books and magazines for student use. Jean Templeman does not write soft. Her written message is harsh, painting a poor image of the school. During her visit, she asked Jean Stevenson what would happen if the school was denied again. What financial impact would it have on the school? What other business interest do I have? What is the makeup of the board? Were we moving soon? Her line of questioning was inappropriate. She was searching. Jean Stevenson informed her she was not involved in the financial aspect of the business. Jean T. wanted to know who else had ownership of the school.

God, You see us – keep us alive.

Today, I met with Linda and Patricia of ASA Learning Center. They provided me with info on Child Care, Domestic Violence, Contracts, Computers, and Food program. I had a meeting with Iris Richardson and Albert Andon regarding the LVN Program. I am seeking to retain referrals. Discussion on the operations of the program, how things developed, the outcome. The door is still open for the school.

I must become more insightful, open to new ideas to grow. Think more. Seek more wisdom. Whatever I lack, I pray. God, provide to assist me in being productive, to maintain the purpose of the school.

Aisha is sorrowful in heart. She feels disconnected with Campus Crusade. The participation of African-Americans is low. I questioned if her presence is what God wants to draw others to Campus Crusade. She is comfortable in the environment and she can be the platform to draw others. I pray for direction for her.

Lord, goodnight.

2/14/2000

Valentine's Day.

Two pies from Alicia, candy from Wendy, and dinner from Ernell. Not bad.

I am thankful to God. Payroll was met, $41,000. We received clearance from ETP for $43,000. Jean is making headway with the VN Program. There are 76 students enrolled. Thirteen will graduate on the 22nd. The ETP is going well with 48 students.

I spoke with Concepcion Powell of CPS Pharmacy. I've been invited to a meeting on Wednesday for contracts. This may be a big breakthrough for us. Tomorrow, I should receive a copy of the Preliminary Plan for the Washington Building. I am excited about the possibilities. Staying in prayer to God for a positive outcome.

I will start to focus on the Friends of Four-D business today. I volunteered to host a 'Pre legal Service Seminar' for Community Outreach. It is scheduled for March 25th at 11:00-12:30.

It was suggested today by Toni Sublim that I write a book. I have much to use, memory and six books of notes. One day.

Lord, thank You for smiling on me!

2/15/2000 ~ 8:45 p.m.

I pray that the Lord binds Jean Templeman up and removes her from our path. Her actions and comments are not in the best interest of the school. She has questioned what would happen if the school did not get the April 17th start. My spirit tells me she is not trustworthy. She has not shared honestly with her Supervisor. She misleads intentionally to cause harm and confusion. I ask God to remove her from our path.

Betty has eight students approved for Rich Canyon Hospital and she scheduled an appointment for me to meet the Director of Beaumont Adult School. I believe God is laying the financial foundation we will need to continue our work.

Linda L. Smith

Tomorrow will be a day full of blessings and financial rewards.

Lord, thank You.

I ordered 100 more books for presentations, and applied for the Children Network Surplus Program. Thanks again.

2/19/2000 ~ 8:45 a.m.

My burden is heavy. I pray to stay encouraged, to stay focused. My eyes are filled with tears of sorrow. I cannot express my thoughts. I clearly see how this path of destruction has come. It is a heartache to have trust in someone when their hidden agenda is to destroy. Jealousy is destructive.

Jean Stevenson has put hundreds of hours addressing the students, faculty needs, and the Nursing Board reports.

My heart is heavy. I feel so uncomfortable with Jean Templeman. I do not believe she acts in the best interest of the school. She has told students to leave; she told Stacy, a student, that I only receive the good evaluations on faculty. The bad ones are discarded by Stephen or the person giving the surveys. She has not been truthful in her presentation with me. I don't know what human form to turn to. I pray to Jesus. I ask that she be removed or that He changes her heart. She is not a person of fairness. Others have suffered the wrath painfully. Every effort is being made to improve communication with the students. I continue to pray.

Yesterday, Yolanda brought the preliminary drawings on 1020 Washington. The total bill is $11,000 for her work. She did her research and produced clear plans with minimum changes. As I look at the plans and I think of the school, I have internal anxiety. *What if we are not approved for an April class? Where will we go? What will we do?* Yolanda, seeing my fear, began to minister to me. Her words were healing. They came following a meeting with Stacy and Julie, 2 students who 'reported' for 45 minutes. Stacy reported about her 45-minute conversation with Jean Templeman. As I listened to her go on and on, I thought to myself, *I am 50 yards from her each day, yet she calls 800 miles to report the school.* She has never had anything to say when I approached her in class.

Yolanda witnessed God's love. Her words reflected my day's journey. I began to cry. She embraced me, holding tight, and I began to pray. She prayed until the pain was gone, the tears had dried, and the focus had returned.

Jean Stevenson, Mr. Peter, and I met to discuss Templeman's report. Mr. Peters gave us focus. Only answer the questions. We spoke with the Wonderlic Ed. Department to obtain translation of codes and numbers. After much discussion and research, Jean and I systematically went through the report. We responded to each question. Jean is much better with the computer than I. She typed and set, I read, prayed, provided verbiage to the questions. Twenty-two pages later, we were done at 11:45 p.m. I faxed the report to Jean T's office. We just pray she decreases and accepts it as meeting the requirement to be on the April 17th agenda. We will know Tuesday.

Following the completion of that task, Jean and I discussed an instructor and our need to make a clinical visit to see the interaction with the students/instruction and to visit the Director of Nurses. At 12:20 a.m., we walked out of the building.

I arrived home at 1:10 a.m. Tired, sleepy. Awakened this morning at 6:00 a.m. by the clock. Ernell and Aisha are going skiing. I lay in bed praying. Overwhelmed, I cried out to God. *I don't know what to do. Why is this happening? I have given according to others. I have been of good service.* I cried for focus, for strength. My faith is strong. I will not tarry. He is with me; there is nothing that can separate me from God.

2/22/2000 ~ 11:07 a.m.

Yesterday, I rose at 6:30 a.m. to listen to the Gospel Station 373. I took my Bible and read, listened to the Word and song. I cried in my hands, tears flowing uncontrollably. Sorrow unexplainable. I felt tormented, lost. I didn't know what to do. I cried and called to God to deliver me. *Show me where to go next. Give me a sign. Give me encouragement.* I prayed He deliver the school from those who want to see destruction. I prayed that He bind Jean Templeman and all others' hearts. I prayed for acceptance of Jean Stevenson's report. As I listen to the Gospel, I took my Bible in hand and began to search for the message back and forth, scanning verses. I came upon Psalms 35 – a prayer for help. I read it over and over. I prayed for help. As I read and prayed, I sought comfort with my Lord.

As I looked at the T.V. Ministry, I received the message and word. I listened to Rev. Morton. His message was, 'Whatever you need, God has it on deposit.' Rev. Randy Morrison spoke on God's ability to master all circumstances. Our perception is not God's. Rev. T.D. Jakes spoke on having favor with God. God is going to bless me. Rev. Hatch spoke on how the promise of God is bigger than the problem. Go from believing in God to believing God. The stories in the Bible tell us the stories. But, Joyce Meyer spoke on peace and how it gives us power. Her demonstration was clear. We should not have spiritual warfare with saints, but stay focused on Jesus. That is the weapon. Satan's evil spirits interfere with our focus on Jesus. If we take our focus off of Jesus to fight Satan, it slows up our production, our work for God. But God will step in to protect us and keep us focused on the Lord. Peace gives us power. I filled my soul with the Word and song. From 6:30-3:00, I was spellbound by the Word. While eating dinner with Ernell and Aisha, I received a call at about 6:00 p.m. Donnie called from Kaiser Hospital. Momma had passed out at home. She was in the ER. I knew immediately in my spirit that she was okay. I started to finish my dinner, but I thought I should get dressed and go right then.

Ernell, Aisha, and I left for the hospital. I came upon my mother with drowsy eyes, tubes connected to her IV, EKG, BP monitors. Donnie and her Nurse, Randy, were putting her back in bed. She had become faint while attempting to get up. All of her tests came back negative. She was dehydrated. I told her the stress of her grown sons was doing this. The lady next to her, Ms. Means, spoke up and said that's why she was in the ER. Her 37-year-old daughter had created a lot of problems for her. But as she said, "I know it is killing me, but what can I do?" I told her I hear her, that was her baby and mothers will take care of their babies until they die. She agreed. I told my mother she will live as long as her grandmother if she relieves herself of some of the stress with her sons. Donnie is back home and Ronnie had bought more of his clothes. He lives in an office in San Diego. *Lord, what is he into?* I called this a.m. She was in bed resting. I am grateful to God for her health and life. I will stay in Spirit, focus on the path. I must go through it to get through it. I will make it with the Lord, my God.

Thank You, Jesus.

Love Your Child in Need,

Linda

2/23/00 ~ 11:50 p.m.

We got a call from Jean Templeman on Tuesday at 5:15 p.m. Jean Stevenson does not take the call. She knows Jean T. is deliberately trying to upset her. Why wait until 5:15 to call? Today, my stomach turned when I heard she was on the line. She is not satisfied with what we had submitted. She picked on one item that was wrong with the program: why we had changed the admission policy without addressing what was wrong with the old policy. Her search for error is haunting. Her language stirs my spirit. I tell her my spirit is telling me she is saying we will not be approved for April. She doesn't deny the statement, but says we have not completely answered question number 5 for the board. Jean Templeman is not acting in our favor.

I spoke with an upset mother, Ms. Mancheres, about her daughter Currie. Why is her daughter failing the VN Program? Currie works 4-12 p.m., full time (Hint Hint). I have a pleasant conversation with Ms. Mancheres. The situation diffused, but before hanging up, she tells me she heard we will not have an April class! Where did she hear that! We talk about monitor visit from several agencies. She tells me she referred her daughter to the Academy because of its reputation. She is aware of the trouble we have had.

Lord, at Conceptions Open House, a Scripture was placed on the wall, from the book of Matthew. 'Having the faith of a mustard seed can move mountains.' My faith is sure. God is surrounding me with faith warriors. I call Lennox Leach. I need to talk privately with Charles Bennett, the President of the Board. Charles works with the State Correction Department.

Lord, help me find him. I do not believe Charles is aware of Jean's tactics. Lennox will try to obtain the telephone number through his contacts. He will also provide me with the number to a Mr. Lloyd Williams, Consultants from Atlanta. He may be able to help or advance me.

I come home and share my concerns with Ernell. Ernell is calm. He tells me everything will work out all right. My tears flow as I share with him God's blessing, my love for what I do. I appreciate his devotion and support. I do pray that the Lord binds Jean T. and removes her or changes her heart. He stresses that meanness is much to bear. God, keep us. Give me wisdom.

Thank You, Lord.

2/24/2000 ~ 11:30

Oh what a blessed day. Bob Rodriguez came to discuss marketing for the Pharmacy Tech Program to obtain a bilingual Tech instructor. Bob shared his family and his love for Jesus. We prayed at the end of our meeting. We prayed for each other's family, business, children, and the school. Oh what a blessing. I called Ann Sherman and requested an appointment to meet with Jean T. Teresa Bello and her ASAP. Lennox Leach provided me the name of Darrell Cooley and Charles Bennett's numbers. I E-mailed Darrell and will speak with him tomorrow. I will call on Charles. Lord, thank You for the prayer warriors. Ernell called me at work to let me know we will make it. I've come too far not to. We will do whatever it takes. His words calmed me and brought tears to my eyes; all I could say was, "Thank you, thank you."

Stephen Byabashaija called at 11:45 p.m. His mother was in a coma. She has not had surgery due to physical state. She is scheduled for kidney surgery. Lord, bless her and family.

2/25/2000 ~ 10:40 p.m.

The saga continues. Jolene is receiving workers comp benefits. She is claiming back injury from her 9/9 fall. She was never off work after returning on Monday 9/13/99. She was terminated 10/11/99. She went to the Doctor 9/13/99. She had more than 6 Doctor visits since 9/13/99. I will submit her job description. I did not receive a call from Ann Sherman to my request to meet with her, Jean Templeman, and Teresa Bello-Jones. We received a notice; we were scheduled for the April 14th agenda and another student complaint was put in their letters. I truly don't understand those who complain for their own failure. Class 8 had a private pre-grad ceremony in their classroom. As I listened to the presentation, I was so pleased to hear the program start with a prayer. The speakers spoke spiritually of God's goodness. Scripture was read from the Bible. Thirteen made it. Many fell by the side in all the turmoil. It was worth it, God is always good. I know they have experienced a life-changing event. They completed a training program. I pray they return to practice the NCLEX review exam. I pray they all pass their boards.

I spoke with Darnell Cooley. I was referred to him by Lenny Leach. I informed Darnell of the circumstances with the Academy. He informed me he would be speaking with members of the Black Caucus. I am to inform him when I am to travel to Sacramento to meet with the 3 Nursing Board representatives.

Jean Stevenson said we might be the one to challenge Jean Templeman to bring change to the board. She should not be allowed to continue to threaten directors. I thought, *Is this God's purpose?* I have been part of change throughout my life. Four-D Success Academy stands for that which is right. Lord, protect us. I spoke with Gary Anday about the Child Care Center at Washington. He was pleased to hear I had not given up. He has information for me regarding state funds for schools with Child Care Centers.

I will be signing for $150,000 line of credit with Bank of America. Pay off the $35,000 to Union Bank.

I will run a bilingual Radio Ad for Pharmacy Tech students by 3/15/2000. God is protecting us.

Thank You, Lord.

2/29/2000 ~ 11:19 p.m.

A busy day – I attended the Mayor of San Bernardino City Breakfast meeting. Within her first sentence, she said, "You have a vision, you will have obstacles. Stay focused." The message comes clear to me. After her presentation, I spoke with her briefly and thanked her. God keeps sending me the message. Michael Williams and I met with the Moreno Valley Gain Office to discuss Work Study Programs, Medical Biller/HCE Pharmacy Tech and other programs. They were very receptive of all of our programs. We expect good relations with them. B of A rep did not come. I called them; he said the contract would be a couple of days. I should see him Tuesday. I signed a contract for a private student. CPS Pharmacy will pay his cost. I spoke with Otis. He says he is trying to come close to the $192,000 figure for the T.I.'s. I just keep praying. Our funding is dropping; the Fed account is at $101,000, ETP (contract) at $91,000, and the savings at $8,000. Lord, keep us. Goodnight.

Linda L. Smith

3/1/2000 ~ 11:26 p.m.

A full day – 9:00 a.m. meeting with Mr. Brown, Beaumont School District and Ken Bonning Gain and Betty Thomas discussion on a partnership to establish a training program. The area is very depressing; hospital (7) is needed. They have about 80 clients ready for training. The District would receive $2,000 for every 525 hours, the Gain office would meet/exceed their quote and we would be able to meet the ETP contract. They are ready to start. Mr. Brown will submit a MOU (Memorandum of Understanding) for my review. We should come to an agreement in seven days once the contract is approved by the school district. We will get started.

I had an 11:00 a.m. appointment with Gary Anday of Riverside County Social Services. He came to measure and discuss the Child Care Center at 1020 Washington. He said I and a center in Waterman Garden were the only ball game in town. He was pleased I was still trying. Gary will mail info for funding assistance. All is well.

1:00 p.m. meeting with Dorothea Williams about Sadiq's book. She will present it to the VP Curriculum Development and Sub-Committee. There is much hope that it will take off. Jean S. and Kaye Hansen were at the office at 6:35 writing on the VN Program. It will be the best when they are done.

The Genius of five Masters Arrival by Donald Brown; Malcolm X, Marcus Garvey, Mahatma Gandhi, Martin Luther King, Mandela. A gift for my husband, Ernell. I suggested that he insure the artwork. It's valued at $4,500.

A good day. Oh, I spoke with Kaiser Manger in Training staff. Good possibility. Lord, thank You.

116

What a blessed Saturday. I attended Campus Crusade Conference at the invitation of Aisha. The conference 'Impact' brought together (African-American), Destino (Mexican) American, and Epic Asian. God was present among these young people. I witnessed praises going up, support and love being exchanged. Open hugs and communication. I met Sue Brior, Margaret, Jan, Michael, Becky, Bobby, James, Kenyetta, and Aleesha. Sue asked me to be a guest speaker at Long Beach State. James White (RN) and I will stay in touch. He is from South Carolina and is interested in training. I stayed over for the banquet. It was a delight. I am so very proud of Aisha. She is blessed and following the path God has for her. As I worked on projects and listened to Gospel, I thought of Jean T. and Ann Sherman. I called Darnell Cooley and left a message to call me. I doubt if he ever contacted Charles. I called Charles' home. No answer. God must be protecting me. I called Donna Bostic. We talked and I expressed my concerns about their action. She explained that I should address the impact of their actions and not their behavior. There is no defense for the impact, but the acts, their behavior, may be misinterpreted by me. I prayed to God. I thought of the Young Women Conference. I project to donate the $10,000 I placed last year. I sat and thought, *I need $210,000. Lord, guide me.* I hear a minister; God does give you the money you need. He anoints the way the money comes to us. I thought, *True.* I think of the city, the Beaumont School District, Moreno Valley, The anointed way God will bring funds needed.

I called Jordan and told her to progress with the plan. April 17th is rapidly approaching. She said God's plan is on time. I am so blessed to be in contact with people who know the Lord. I am blessed. Four-D Success Academy will have a new home by June 7, 2000.

We claim God's gift of 1020 Washington, Colton. Lord, we will maintain it in the spirit of Your love.

Thank You. Jesus.

3/6/2000 ~ 7:15 a.m.

Dressed and ready for work, I glanced at my Bible on the floor. I stopped with the thought, *Let me get fed.* I asked God to show me His Word, what I need. I opened the Bible and turned to Psalms 37. *Trust in the Lord.* I read it and the tears came. Ernell was present. He listened. '*Do not fret because of evildoers...Trust in the Lord, and do good. Rest in the Lord. Do not fret - it only causes harm. For the Lord upholds him with His hand.'* As I read the verses, I knew God directed me to this chapter. Yesterday, I fretted - I wanted to talk with Charles Bennett, with Darnell Cooley, with Donna. I needed to seek help. I was fretting over Jean Templeman's wrongdoing.

Last evening, I spoke with Yolanda. As we talked about the building, she said, "God's plan is coming together. Don't worry (fret)." Lord, continue to bless us, protect us from harm. Trust in the Lord. He sees all. Continue to do good work. Continue to do good work. Trust in the Lord.

Jesus, thank You for these words. I needed them this day. I will stay focused on the school and let You work with me.

3/6/2000 ~ 10:57 p.m.

Stephen B. was due back to work on February 28th - thus far, no call, no show. I spoke with Charlie Seymour, Chair of Advisory Board. Charlie recommend that I send an e-mail to Stephen informing him of his termination from the company and that I should change the passwords Stephen used.

I E-mailed Darnell Cooley. The results were positive. Teresa Bello-Jones, Executive Director of the Board, called me at 2:30 p.m. We discussed my concerns of Jean Templeman, the March 21st meeting. She requested Jean Stevenson speak only with Ann Sherman. Teresa will call back next Tuesday.

I called Lenny Leach to thank him for his assistance. Tomorrow, I will call Darnell.

I approved the MOU with Beaumont District. It will go before the Board for approval. We both expect a positive outcome. This morning, I read Psalm 37 – *Trust in the Lord.*

I spoke with Duneen DeBuhurl. I requested her support for the principle presentation on April or March. She agreed.

Robert Rochelle came to the office to see me. He prayed. Lord, what a blessed, wonderful gift his prayers and words were. He asked if I had applied for the new contract. I didn't know it was out. I had one by the end of the day. It is due Friday at 5:00 p.m. I will deliver.

Lord, thank You.

-Moreno Valley Presentation last week.

-Beaumont School District MOU Contract.

-South Bay Contract due Friday.

-City of San Bernardino screening for 10-15 students.

-Kaiser Hospital seeks training for 6 medical billers.

-SB County proposal due Friday.

-Riverside County will open up. Thank You, Lord.

3/7/2000 ~ 11:36

Stephen has not called since February 24th. He is 7 days past his return date. I e-mailed him on 3/2. It was read 3/4. I issued official notice of termination effective immediately. Steps will be taken to change the password. I will discontinue his e-mail.

Iris Richardson called to give her support. She said she was led by the Lord to call me. She read Psalm 47:1-9. I was so moved. God continues to send His messages, His gift of prayer. Yolanda picked up the plans and her check. She is moving ahead. Otis should have prices within the next day or two.

I pray for peace, organization, productivity, and high revenue for us all. I pray for a positive net income at June 30, 2000.

Lord, thank You.

3/8/2000 ~ 11:35 p.m.

"KEYS TO 1020 WASHINGTON"

Oh happy day! I was handed the keys to our suite. I held them in my hand, rolled them through my fingers. I thought, *My God, the reality is close.* Otis, John, and I viewed the 1st floor again. Otis has recommendations to improve the plans. I like them. I thought I was going to get the plans and cost today for the bank, but it will be another 7-10 days.

Escrow closes on April 17. I need $200,000 Lord. I will wait to see how it will come together.

He knows I just need to keep on. Pressing on. Faith on. Focus on.

Thank You, Lord.

3/9/2000 ~ 11:10 p.m.

Working on proposals for SB County and S Bay Plc. Lord, bless us with contracts. Spoke with Ernest Dowdy and received congratulations on the success of the City of San Bernardino recognizing Four-D Success as an independent employment and training entity. Good lunch today with Ben Cortes, rep with Assemblyman Longwille. We spent 3 hours together 11:30-2:30. We both enjoyed the company.

I spoke with Yolanda. The plans will be redone. She will come to the house Monday a.m. I spoke with Joy at the bank. Plans needed to boost the price, although she is telling me the price. The appraisal is okay; just want to present a 'complete package' to the board.

Five weeks and Escrow closes. LORD, there is much to do between now and June 7th. Keep us focused.

I worked until 9:00 p.m. Had to complete those proposals for Wendy. Much to do tomorrow. Thank You, Lord.

Certified letter marked to Stephen. We move on.

3/10/2000 ~ 7:15 a.m.

Awakened at 6:00 I lay and prayed to my Lord. I prayed for protection for the school, financial protection, staff protection, family protection. I listened to the ministry on T.V. I spoke with my husband on the Word of God and trusting in Him, being in agreement with the desires of our heart. Trusting in God. Stop blocking the blessing coming from God. We had wanted to build onto our house BUT we blocked God's blessing. We did not come into agreement on the house. We did not pray for it. I wanted it - we did not agree. His desire for a boat - we did not agree. I heard Rev.

Copeland say he never uses the words, "I can't afford it." God Can. Ernell and I prayed to be in agreement. I prayed for us, for him, our business. We prayed to be in agreement and to trust in God. I then went to Aisha and prayed with her. God is preparing her. We were in agreement that she is an intelligent being and God will have her to learn languages to spread His Word. We agree in His blessing.

Lord, thank You for Your messages and for Your Word.

3/11/2000 ~ 8:30 a.m.

Yesterday, I signed a contract with K-Cal Radio, Robert Zamora, Hispanic station. Robert is willing to aid the school in enrolling Hispanic students. I know we will double or triple the Hispanic enrollment at the school. Marcus and Keema Houston have been hired to work with my Financial Aid Department as consultants. God has truly brought this together.

Keema and I met in Bible class. She was engaged to Mark (Cherry's ex-husband). I/we were not able to work together due to the stained relationship between Cherry and Mark, but now God brings us together for the good of Four-D Success Academy.

We submitted a proposal contract to SB County. Wendy and I worked on it and it was delivered at 5:29 p.m. The doors were locked at 5:30. Just at that time, Dr. Henry and Lawrence drove up. I looked at the County staff and said, "I know you are not going to lock Dr. Henry out, not Dr. Henry." They unlocked the door and allowed Lawrence to deliver his package. I shared my words with Dr. Henry after Lawrence had checked in his proposal. We all laughed. She said, "God is going to bless you for that. We contracted last year. They may not give me one this year. But I know you will get one. They had to let you in." She repeated God's blessing to come to Four-

D Success. I joyfully wait for a signed contract. The Lord has blessed us to stay together. He continues to move people out and bring Believers in who sincerely want to help the school. I pray for people who know and love the Lord, and are of good spirit. God will (is) blessing those who help the school. This I know with all of my heart.

Jesus, thank You for loving me, for loving the Academy, and for loving my family. I pray for my brothers. I pray for their release from drugs and alcohol. I pray that they give up foolishness. I pray that they seek You, ask for forgiveness, ask for healing, ask that You, Heavenly Father, come into their life. I pray that they accept Jesus as their Lord and Savior.

I pray for my mother's peace and strength. I thank God for the love she has for her children. I pray for Momma's endurance. Lord, take care of Momma. I can only pray for her. A mother's love for a child cannot be measured by another. I only can pray for salvation.

3/12/2000 ~ 8:36 a.m.

Good morning, Lord. Today Bishop G.E. Patterson taught on "No one can stop God's plan for you (me)." Whatever God's plan is, it is unstoppable by another. And then Pastor Leroy Thompson...

A) Money does not pay your bills off. The anointing of God brings the money to me – four principles.

Matthew 6   1) Keep God first.

Stewardship   2) God owns everything; I own nothing.

3) God is first, others second, me last.

4) God is my source.

The Lord will bless the school with not only the money we need for the school, but God will bless Four-D Success with the $10,000 for the Young God's Women Conference. It will be because God said so! He has blessed my seed to give unconditionally.

Lord, thank You for the financial blessing.

3/13/2000 ~ 9:15 p.m.

Today, Yolanda and I went over the plans for 1020 Washington. I am pleased. I sat and watched her make drawings come alive with her laptop computer. The shape, dimension, walls, sinks were all there. I could see it. We talked about God's blessings. Yolanda is so positive. She keeps saying in her Jamaican accent, "Don't worry, everything is going to work out fine. See, City Planning knows you. You have the plans for the bank. Otis will give you the costs. You will be out and moved by the first of June." She tells me to let people know what I am doing. I have a testimony. I express my concerns about the negative spirits. I don't want anyone praying against me. She understands.

"April 17th, escrow closes. Then, I can really talk."

Yolanda said, "Who knows, there may be someone who wants to furnish the whole place – just because they like what you are doing." Now, that would be something. But all things are possible.

I signed the papers for $150,000 line of credit. Paid off Union Bank for $34,000. $115,000 available.

The letter went to staff. Stephen B. is no longer on staff. I finally used the correct words for his action: abandonment. My tears/confusion flowed yesterday. Today is a new day. I cleared his office on Saturday – deleted his e-mail and AOL today. We press on. Tomorrow, Otis and I will meet. I will fax the Child Care Plans to Gary Andoy. We move on.

I am so sleepy. I am seldom in bed by 9:00 p.m. 3 hours ahead of my normal time.

Goodnight, Lord.

3/14/2000 ~ 10:04 p.m.

God answered prayers.

I met with Otis Lacey, Contractor, at B.C. Café to discuss the plans for 1020 Washington, Colton. We discussed the layout use of tile vs. carpet, types of doors. We also discussed doing good deals for others and faith. Otis assures me everything will work out.

At work, Ann Logan informs me that Stephen called for her, using the name of Jason. He wants to meet with her. He asked her how she was doing and if she would meet him after work. She thinks he is up to something. Caution to be taken in answering questions. I requested she not reveal anything to him.

Call from Teresa Bello-Jones and Ann Shuman. Teresa started out by saying, "They are there to help the school and to make sure everyone is treated fairly." Jean Stevenson is to report only to Ann Shuman. The recommendation to the Board is to approve the start of 45 students for the April 17th class. The instructional plan needs some minor changes. We need to obtain another acute hospital, but they would not hold up class for April. I informed them that Jean S. and I would not need to travel to Sacramento. I once again expressed my view of the truth. The consultant relation with staff dismissed from the school and their role in collaborating against the school.

I called the staff to the conference room. I informed them of the "good" news. I thanked them for their support and we were led in prayer by Sheryl Williams. We cheered and we thanked God. I thanked them for their support, for not leaving Four-D Success. Lord, thank You.

I spoke with Anthony Lopez, Administrator of Beaumont Convalescent Care. He is anxiously waiting to have the CNA Program at his facility. I spoke with Ken (GAIN in Banning). He has 5 facilities seeking our services. God continues to bless us. Mike informed me the current owner needed the bank's approval to sell the building to me and they hadn't talked with the leasee in the Family Connection Center. Mike was calm. Things will work out. I informed Ernell of the day's events. He was happy. I could see him smiling over the telephone. Charlie questioned Stephen's actions. He says Stephen thought we were going to fail. God cleared house. Stephen was removed, we press forward. I am so thankful to God. He protects us against those we do not know.

Lord, thank You.

I pray for the revenue to have $200,000 for the escrow, $10,000 for Young God's Women Conference YGWC, reminded to exceed the 10% we require for the 90/10 ratio. I pray for the Beaumont Contract, the start of the CNA Program for the City, SB County Contract, and Riverside County Contract. 100 students each in the Medical Building/HCE and Pharmacy Tech Program and expansion of the CNA Program. Lord, grant us this blessing. Thank You.

3/16/2000 ~ 7:23 p.m.

I sit and think of God.

His blessings are all and all. As we near the date to close escrow, I examine where we have come. It's a long way from 1992 and 2 students. God has brought us far. So much has happened. Growth has brought happiness, joy, concerns, trust, disappointments, surprises, tears, prayers, faith, and leaning on the Lord.

Many chapters have been closed. The story goes on. The latest chapter was the departure of Stephen. He came in on Wednesday to get his belongings. I chose not to greet him. There was nothing to say. I didn't want to give another minute of my time to his stories/situation. We move on.

Today, I shared with the management team the plans to consolidate the classes/room. We did a master schedule. I pray God prepares us all, that we are wise in our decisions and plans, and that we work together for the good of Four-D Success Academy.

The current owner has not provided the adjustment line (lot) for the escrow. I became concerned. The tenet had not been informed of the move. I was concerned, but Mike says not to worry. But God, my God, knows where we stand. April 17, 2000, Escrow closes. Tears well up in me. My chest heaves. Joy, excitement. I, Linda Smith, have come far. My faith is my base. My belief in God's will for my life. Four-D Success Academy is the sounding board of what my life is and is to be according to God's will. I fear not. As we prepare to move forward, I see God's groundwork for advancement: computerized programs, new healthcare programs, contracts not imagined, students in the thousands, double faculty, and booming Child Care Center.

Matthew informed me he has been approached frequently by Cherry to work with her. He wanted to know if there was enough work for him to work full-time with our computers or he would do split time between us.

Matthew is so nervous in his speech and presentation. I inform him his choice is fine with me. He will not work between the two. Cherry's ethics and spirit do not parallel with mine. I would be perfectly okay with his decision. I am absolutely at ease and okay if he leaves. God already has a replacement. The Financial Aid Department is holding. We do have work to do. But everything will be all right. God is my all and all.

Lord, guide us. Protect us. Open the door for us.

3/17/2000 ~ 11:15 p.m.

I have felt lazy and slow all day. At one point, I thought I was boring. Aisha and I went to the Ontario mall. My joy, buying 6 bras. She was shopping for her getaway to Compton – Campus Crusade retrieval. I didn't want to drive anywhere, I didn't want to see anyone, I didn't want to eat, and I didn't want to talk with Ernell. I felt empty, unsure of the reasons. Life is funny. I undressed and laid on the couch, dozing, and got a telephone call. I rose, dressed, and chatted briefly with Ernell.

Tomorrow, Tahira is off for 2 weeks of training. I need a life outside of work. But I don't know what to do. I think it is time for biological changes. In a couple of days, I will be fine. Today is the 17th – one month to close escrow. My God, help us. I am going to sleep. Tomorrow, I will feel great.

Thank You, Lord.

3/20/2000 ~ 10:49 p.m.

I went to 1020 Washington for lunch and prayer. A subway sandwich, chips, and coke. I entered the building with MY key. As I entered, I felt blessed and excited. Placing my lunch on the receptionist counter, I began to imagine the office, staff, furniture, wall décor. I entered my office, opened the blinds, and looked out. I could see my parking space from my window, the bathroom in the corner, furniture. The assistant's space, I counted off 9 feet by 10 feet. The director's office, too small, could hold a desk, chairs, and plants. Where will the Accounting Department go? Plenty of room. I walked, prayed, walked, looked, prayed, thanked God, and I returned to my office. A call from Otis Lacy, contractor. We discussed the cost, the need to provide the bank with figures. He and I will meet tomorrow at 9:00 a.m. I have the plans ready. The bank will receive both tomorrow. Within 30 minutes, I received a call from Michael Ballard. He had been in contact with the owner. They are moving on the property line adjustment, the relocation of the tenant. He will keep in contact weekly. I spoke with Les Coplin and requested a 30-day extension on the Cooley lease. He inquired about the move, the sale price. I laughed and told him I would not reveal the sale price until papers were signed.

Ernell informed me he had put in for $45,000 from his contract value. The line of credit was approved for $155,000. I have $115,000 available. We will start a CNA/HHA class with 9 students on Wednesday the 28th. We can bill after 10 days for $11,000. We will earn $45,000 by June 1st, this will help the 90/10 ratio.

Donnie (brother) called me. I was told Dr. Duneen DeBruhl; the editor for the history book will order slips. She will love them. Lord, the door is opening. Goodnight.

3/21/2000 ~ 10:30 p.m.

Sometimes it seems as though it will never end. God continues to reveal individuals who do not have the Academy's interest at heart. Last Friday, after the management meeting, Matthew Elbert, secretary, informed me he was being sought by Cherry for employment. I informed him he could leave because I would not accept part-time nor a co-business relationship with her or him. He informed me I would have his decision if he chose to leave. Monday afternoon, he emailed Cherry and she responded. He is using FDSA time and expense to work for her. He will be terminated due to conflict of interest on Wednesday.

3/21/2000 ~ 10:30 p.m.

I received the proposal, contractions, and estimates from Otis. The cost for the TI's and the plan along with the Lease Agreement between FDSA, Inc. Ernell and I were submitted to Business Bank of California. The adjustment property line and the approval plans by the City will close the deal. The appraisal will come in at the required amount. We will move on time.

I praise God for this blessing, direction, protection. I pray for focus and endurance. I pray for staff who loves Christ, who will devote their time to help others, pray with students. I pray for continuance of doing good work.

I just thank Jesus.

Thank You, Lord.

3/23/2000 ~ 6:51 a.m.

Yesterday was Matthew Elbert's, Secretary to DON, last day with the school. He had been warned not to work for Cherry on the school's time. Last Friday, he informed me of his continued loyalty to her, and it cost him his job. He seemed quite surprised when Jean S. and I entered his office. I requested his keys and informed him that due to his conflict in interest and continued work with Cherry, he was terminated. I had proof of e-mails from 3/20 and 3/21. As he started to sign the exit interview form, he hesitated and commented, "I don't quite understand," and then he signed. Matthew boxed his things. I turned off his computer. He said goodbye to some members and left the school. I spoke with Wendy, Ann Logan, and Margie. I was concerned about them reacting to his dismissal. They were not surprised. Matthew had expressed his dislike of the school and had become very vocal about wanting to leave. Each lady shared their conversations with him. They knew it was "individual" unavoidable. Afterwards, I spoke privately with Wendy. She expressed her view of my reasons for paying certain persons big dollars and they 'literally screw me without Vaseline.' Cherry and Stephen were paid as top executives before they left the company. The staff that stayed and helped keep the company together were paid far less. I listened and informed Wendy I had developed a pay scale for staff. In June/July I would inform everyone. I ask that she inform me of my actions if she feels I am going off-base. I lack a supportive sounding board. She agreed. I know I will be better. I will assess where we stand financially and make wage adjustments. A 10% across the board increase is a good start. We will press forward to continued success.

God, keep us together.

Yolanda informed me the Architectural Plans will be ready by next Wednesday 3/29 for the City of Colton. Keep us on track, Lord.

This day is blessed by God.

3/23/2000 ~ 11:24 p.m.

I spoke with Eric at U.S. Department Education in San Francisco. The ETP CNA/HHA Program will be approved as an eligible program. This will allow the Academy to meet the 90/10 rule. I gleamed with joy. Lord, thank You.

I spoke with Dr. Duneen DeBruhl. She presented the book to the Principals. It went well...better than well. Judy White, V.P. Superintendent of School, has requested an order form. She is over the City of Readers Program. This book is going to take off. We move forward.

Tomorrow, I am to obtain the keys to the building and door – which I did not receive originally to the electrical panel and restroom. Each day is another day closer.

3/24/2000 ~ 11:21 p.m.

Appraisal at $1.9 million. I received the word – the appraisal on 1020 E Washington came back at $1.9 million. We qualify for the loan. The only things needed are the approved plans and God's check for $192,000 by April 17th. I am glad He has the money! This evening from 6-10:00, I was at the Double Tree in Ontario. I am on the tape ministry. We labeled 1,000 tapes for Tomorrow's Day Extraordinary. An estimate 1,000 ladies are expected.

Lord, thank You for this day.

God's Woman Conference at the Double Tree Hotel – Ontario, CA

Oh what a blessed day! I worked the tape ministry, blessing women who wanted to take the messages of the day and yesterday with them. At the beginning of the first session, I decided to go into the Conference Room. Charlene Singleton was speaking. The gathering of over 1,000 women was involved in song, praise, and prayer.

Beatrice Gardiner. Lord, what can I say? 1,000 women filled the room, ladies in every seat, along the wall, in the hallway, and at the door. Beatrice was ministering to the souls. She began to prophesy to individuals. I stood in the back, hands and arms extended high above my head. I felt as though I've never lifted my arms so high. I felt as though I was touching God. High above my head, I felt something.

I looked towards Beatrice. I turned my head away. She doesn't see me. I felt God's presence. Beatrice continued to pray for different women in the back of the room, the one with her arms and hands held over her head. Who is it? The crowd wondered, *Is it me?* She says, "You, in the bone top. Are you sitting or standing?" She is speaking to me. Out of the crowd – out of 1,000, in the back of the room – Beatrice called me. She told me to come forward. I felt the Lord. As I moved through the crowd, down the aisle, she told me to stop midpoint. She told me God is sending a message, and that 21 days from this day, it will be over. Not to worry. That which I need is done. I shout, leap, point to her, cry, jump, shout. That's it, that's it. My mind races – what is today's date? What is 21 days from this date? How many days in this month? It is April 14th. 21 days from this date. God has sent a message. 21 days from this date. April 14,

Linda L. Smith

2000 – the Prophet spoke to me. The Nursing Board will approve the VN Class. God has stepped in. He has made everything all right. The building she spoke of is the building God has picked for the school. There was a good word for me, a message from God. Following the praise service, I returned to the tape counter. I sought my calendar. I counted back from April 14th to March 25th. 21 days. The LORD had spoken to me. Tears in my soul cried out and the Lord heard my cry. He felt my pain for the school and the students. He protects us. Those who sought to harm the school will not prosper. Their greed will consume them. Their wallets will never be filled. Dissatisfied, they will always be. Lord, I thank You. Thank You for this message. I wish no harm to another. I pray for their well-being. I pray that they seek You – that they seek forgiveness for wanting to harm Your school, Your students, and Your child. I pray that they seek prayer to forgive themselves. Lord, thank You for my husband, daughters, mother, and brothers. Thank You for all You have done. Thank You for Your forgiveness. Thank You for Your love. I came home and shared the good news with Ernell and Aisha. I told them about the prophecy. I told them about God's blessing. I told them they must listen to the tape. God spoke through Beatrice to me. I told them of the 21 days. 21 days, Lord, 21 days.

He spoke to me through Beatrice Gardiner. Jesus, thank You.

3/26/2000 ~ 7:33 a.m.

I awakened with tears. God's blessing is on me. I am under the veil of His blessings. The school is protected, I cried. I dreamed I was at a counter eating. Opposite of me was Cherry Houston. Her demeanor was quiet, not loud and boastful as usual. Her hair had lost its blondness, her face had no joy, it was shaped thin, and I didn't recognize her body. She expressed her difficulties. She lost her car;

134

she was working for Home Health Registry. She wasn't making the money she needed to keep going, left FDSA $80,000. I could only listen, no comment, no sorrow. God is. I called Momma to share the prophecy.

3/28/2000 ~ 11:10 p.m.

The Revolution Fest 2000. Tonight Loveland had its first annual Revolution for Christ Festival. It was held at the Ontario Convention Center. The lively singers were praising the Lord, lifting up the Spirit. I raised my arms and envisioned embracing the 1020 Washington Building. It was gently pressed against my bosom, my head resting against the east side looking south. I was happy again. "This is mine, God gave me this." I can serve many students and pray for them. I was so comfortable embracing all that God had given me. Moments later, Kirk, the lead singer, told the audience to see and hold what they wanted from God! I had already done so. Lord, I had already done so!

As Pastor Chuck delivered the word from Acts 14:14-22, he explained that "Christ" is the anointing. He, Jesus Christ, is anointed upon Jesus. We are anointed in Christ. The Church is anointed. The Church must (needs to) anoint the Word. Spread the Word. He asked who wanted to be part of the revolution, who wanted to financially support the Revolution — Sudan for Christ? I rose and began to pray. Asked God to answer my heart. He has given me Four-D Success Academy. That is my work. I prayed that God financially bless the Academy, allow it to provide the financial support to the Ministry. I prayed to support Aisha in her work, the Church, the school. It left this warm, burning spot in the center of my chest. A glow within, no pain, no discomfort, but warm, glowing. I prayed, I submitted unto the Lord. God is blessing me through the Academy. He will bless us financially to provide support to other ministries. Today, *Dr. Duneen DeBruhl* prayed for me in her office at Rio Vista. God continues to show himself. Keep encouraged.

He has delivered. I must go through the process. April 14th, the Board approval; April 17th Escrow closes. He is able to do all things. Lord, thank You for this blessed day. Thank You. This evening, I prayed with (for) Aisha: A husband who knows the Lord, a helpful mate who wants a permanent relationship and family, a financial support for her and the children to come. We prayed for financial blessing, to allow her the total freedom to live life financially free of worry. We prayed for a best friend, one who knows and loves the Lord, one she can share her deepest thoughts/secrets to. A friend to laugh, cry with, a friend of interest, fun. Someone who will share life, a lifetime buddy. Male or female, although a female is more preferred. We pray to God for those things. We pray to God for answered prayer. We prayed to God because we believe. We prayed to God to bind Satan and his workers up, bind and cast them away from God's children. We bind Satan out of our hearts, minds, souls, spirits. We bind in the anointed bind of Jesus. I know God hears and answers prayer. He answers prayers.

Lord, thank You.

3/30/2000 ~ 9:32 a.m.

Exhausted emotionally, exhausted physically, distraught spiritually. Overwhelmed. Prayers have been coming my way. God is sending his angels, Satan stays on track. But God is good. Heavily laden, I swell with sorrow, pain. I am weary. I stand. I fight. I pray. I stand. The past two days have moved me. On Monday, I met with the architect to measure the building. He was not aware that I was promised plans on Friday. He doubts that I will have them, but he would speak with the person in charge. Lord, let there be no delays. Ms. Templeman continues to shed the cloth of evil. She writes the history of the school for the Board. This does not occur for any other school. I have prayed to God, ask that He bind her and remove her. I feel the negative spirit in her soul. God's wrath should be upon her. I know Satan uses her; he can't stand the praying going up to God; he can't stand the praying for the staff and the students; he will use anyone he can to stop the prayers to God. We will not cease.

Tuesday and Wednesday, I attended the Revolution Spring Fest with Loveland Church and Pastor Rod Parsley. It was a blessing both nights. Pastor Parsley preached on the "Breakthrough to Jesus," and the Spirit of the Lord was upon us, Four-D Success Academy. Lord, I need a breakthrough. I have planted financial seeds. I have planted prayers. I have planted tears, all in request to Jesus.

This morning, while lying in bed, I began to pray. As I prayed, I felt the bowels of my soul cry out, scream out to Jesus for help. Uncontrollably, I repeated the cries for help. From the depth of my bowels, with the soul of my voice, I called out to Jesus for help. Hear my cry, oh Lord. Deliver us. We need You. Keep the students in the school. Make our telephone ring off the hook. Flood our classrooms with students, and have students to repay loans 100%. Keep the staff in place. Lord, let no one lose their job. I cried out to Jesus, Jesus, Jesus. My soul is aching for the Lord. I cried that He speak to me. Let me hear His voice, call me by name.

I have done all I can. Forgive me of my mistakes, give me wisdom, give me direction, and light the path You want me to travel. Let me be a good steward of those things You have assigned to me. I cried out to Jesus for help. Clear the path. Put us on top of the plateau. Lord, raise us up on your wings. Bind Satan and his works. Keep us, oh Lord Jesus. I cried out to my Lord. My heart aches. I will continue to stand fast for the Lord. I will continue to work for Four-D Success Academy. I will continue to pray for the school, the staff, and the students. The Lord will be in our presence. I prayed for every chair, table, file cabinet, trash bin, paper clip. I prayed for the new building: the carpet, stairs, installations, door, chair, students, staff, telephone, mail, and cement. I prayed for students, the Child Care Center, and the kids. I prayed for the light, light fixtures, the grass, the water, the student lounge, the refrigerator, the beds, books, training equipment, windows, and roof. I prayed for financial blessing. I prayed that the school support the ministry of those who will travel the world to spread the Gospel of Jesus Christ. I prayed to have enough to donate in the years to come. I know God can. I prayed that each staff member have the desires of their heart. I prayed to pay more in wages at least $3 more per hour per person. I pray that God unleash all the hold on the school, students, staff, and those who will come to help. I pray that God will only send those who love Him. I pray for blockage of wrongdoers. I pray for a covenant of protection. The wolf in sheep clothing comes to steal. I pray for a deeper spirit of discernment, a spirit to recognize the wrong of others and the spirit of deception. Lord, I pray for a breakthrough.

3/31/2000 ~ 11:00 p.m.

I rose to go to work feeling better emotionally. Yesterday, I had to spend time alone with the Lord. It was a day to come up from the well. I had been feeling overwhelmed by the events of the past year. People do change. Those that I thought I could trust, I couldn't. Sheep clothing. The school's needs, the student's needs, the faculty's needs. I was drowning (I thought) in caring for everyone but me. Last Saturday, I took a good look at myself. I am fat, out of shape. I have not eaten oatmeal in more than six months. Nowhere to go, I'm bored. The school has become my major focus. I felt drained, used by people I trusted and complaining students. I was tired. I had to seek God. I had to come out of the well. I had a TALK with God. I asked Him to see me, see the pain, see my efforts to do all I could with the school. I asked God to help me stay focused, to strengthen me. I cried out for help. I prayed He bind the consultant and all others who desire to hinder the school's progress.

Today, Mariana (Med Society) informed me she was leaving to work in Euclid Property Management in Upland. We were offered the oven/stove. We are excited to receive it for the new site. Otis Lacy called to inform me he had doors, frames, and possible air conditioners for the new site. Lord, thank You. A brighter, better day.

Linda L. Smith

Looking Back...

- A lifelong student is one that perseveres to consistently educate their mind in a concerted effort to add value and substance to the life of others. By example, I strive to evolve as a person in my personal life, career, and business — it's an ongoing life of learning.

- Sticking to foundational principles that garner success are mainstays to my life and business. Prayer has always been a personal tool for me and the stability around the Four-D family, and will always be.

- It takes teamwork to really make the dream work. The energy of all those involved in the operation of the business must be united and cohesive for positive results to be seen.

- Our reactions to the dictates of life are best defined by our response to the unexpected. Decide to choose peace and pursue it, and the outcomes in your life will be more favorable.

- Purposely creating a space to allow wisdom to come forth is essential to preparing for the success you crave.

- It's not enough to educate yourself; one must apply the information received in every aspect of your life for progress to take shape.

- Never be afraid to ask for what you want. *You have not because you ask not.*

Listen, people will change their minds. When they do, their indecisiveness should not shake your foundation too much. If it does, that means you were too dependent upon them to solidify the dream and vision you had for yourself in the first place. Do what you were commissioned to do, pray that the Lord will send committed people to assist you in your assignments, and He will.

Business by Faith

Journal 7

Begins: April 2, 2000 ~ 11:59 p.m.

Ends: December 18, 2000 ~ 10:41 p.m.

4/2/2000 ~ 11:59 p.m.

Today, Ernell and I met Otis and Avendel at the school. They brought 14 doors and frames to me for the new site. This saved the Academy 50% on the cost of doors. They had loaded the doors in Pasadena on Saturday along with other furniture. I offered to pay for the U-Haul truck, but Otis told me not to worry about it. Following their departure, Ernell and I moved the donated oven to the school's lounge. I guess we received a $150 (used) donation. If I had to purchase these items new, it possibly would have cost approximately for each door ($285 x 14) = $3,990 and the oven at $500 for a grand total of $4,490.00. My $500 seed to give is being rewarded.

Later in the day, I drove to Moreno Valley to purchase shoes. On the way back, I drove to 1020 Washington to pray. I entered the building, walked to the hallway, and placed my purse and keys on the counter. As I raised my hand to receive Jesus, I began to pray for the Academy, staff, and students. I placed my hands on the walls and began to pray for the much-needed financial breakthrough. I prayed to Jesus to protect the students, to guide the school, to instill the desire for excellence in the staff. I prayed for the Child Care Center, the children to come, the staff. I prayed for financial balance. I prayed God would remove all obstacles that strive to hinder the school's progress and work. I prayed for forgiveness of my sins. I thanked God for blessing me with the Academy. I prayed for the City Planning Department, excellent cooperation to approve the plans. I prayed for victory. I thanked Jesus for His grace, kindness, for keeping the school going. I prayed for people to come that love the Lord. I prayed that I could identify wolves in sheep clothing. I prayed for protection. I thanked Jesus for all and all.

Tomorrow will be a blessed day with the Lord, my family, the school, and for me. Lord, thank You for everything.

4/4/00 ~ 10:54 p.m.

I spoke with Joe, property manager of 1020 Washington. I had to hear, firsthand, what was going on. Why was it taking so long to release the property? I was informed that the owner of Safeco did not want to separate the properties, but Joe felt it would happen. Their agent has told them it is in everyone's best interest. The Family Connection had not approved of a new location, but felt that it would not be a problem. The Lot Line Adjustment has gone to the city. I expressed to Joe my current situation. I had nowhere to go! I had been waiting since Jan/Feb. Nothing was solid. I requested his assistance and asked that he keep me informed. My heart sank for 2-5 seconds. Then I said, "No! I will not stop! I will not be shaken. I have work to do." I began making calls and scheduling appointments. I continued to pray for favor of the management of Safeco. Faith and determination keep me going.

Lord, thank You.

4/5/2000 ~ 11:00 -12:00 p.m.

Today, I met with Judy, V.P. Special Education of SB County School. I presented Sadiq's book. The meeting was successful. She will order 20 books for the Principal's meeting scheduled for April 18th. I will ask Dr. Duneen DeBruhl to present it for me. Judy will also include the book in the next grant she writes. The goal is to obtain funds to provide the book on a large scale to the elementary/middle school kids. I will continue to press forward. I made an appointment to meet with Ms. Sanchez with the County School at Judy's suggestion. It is good to have support and networking contacts. Ken and I met at the City Planning Office. He will need to present easement level plans by Monday. The plans will be presented to the Planning Commission on April 17th at 4:00 p.m. Escrow is scheduled to close on that day. I notified Jay at Business Bank of California of the current status. I still need to present the January financials and the signed contract between Otis, Lacy, and I for the tenant improvements. Jay is very positive; the approved loan will not be affected. The escrow will close after the plans are approved and the property is separated. I spoke with Dr. Pastor Turner of the Church of the Living God in LA. He is employed with the VA Hospital in LA. I had placed a call to him seeking equipment needs: beds, weight scales, linen, hood, Hoyer lifts, etc.

He said the timing was good. He said he could get the things I requested and he would store them for us until they're needed. God's plan is in place. I must stay focused. I hired Donnie to work on my computers. I had been in prayer as to whether or not to hire him. He is off probation; I talked with him and explained the environment. No smoking, no friends on site, no cursing. He needs the work. He has the skills. It will be good for his self-esteem. I pray he performs above my expectations. I informed Ernell of my actions. He had no comments. Therefore, I assume he is okay with it.

I drove to the new site Saturday in my car and prayed to God. I prayed that Safeco release the building, the city approve the plans, and that we move forward with the school. We must move into our new home on time. God answers prayers. I breathe with such ease and peace. I am doing the best I can. I will always do the best I can. Lord, thank You.

A new volume begins. So much has happened since I began writing my thoughts back in 1991. Nine years. It has been said that if you think about writing a book, then you should write it. I have been asked many times throughout the years to do that very thing. I do have a story to tell. Trials, tribulations, victories, jubilation, sorrow, tears, laughter, dedication, and pursuit to achieve. I am not the brightest, but I pray for wisdom to excel in the direction God wants me to go. I will take wisdom any day over intelligence. A smart fool is not what I desire to be. Wisdom leads me to the rock that is greater than I. It is there that I find my direction and answers.

Yesterday, I met with Otis, Lacy, the contractor for 1020 Washington. We reviewed the plans. I was informed of changes, provided advice on cost-saving measures. We spent about 3 hours at the Donut Shop discussing business, religion, and plans for the future and our personal business. I ended the evening having dinner with Ernell at the Olive Garden. Life is good. Aisha spent the night on Saturday at Tahira's house. My heart was happy – my daughters together, friends, caring for one another. God has blessed my family.

Tomorrow, I will call Joe Lacko about the building. I expect a positive outcome.

I saw Arlene at Church today. She cheerfully asked what day it was. She was counting down to 21. She informed me she was praying for me and the blessed outcome. God has many prayer warriors for the school and me.

I received the proof that Stephen Byabashaji attended the African Summit. He doesn't deserve unemployment benefits for lying. But that is not for me to determine. I will submit the information to the Gratification Center tomorrow. Lord, thank You for this blessed day.

4/10/2000 ~ 11:18 p.m.

Today, I met Pete, the architect for the 1020 building. He, Yolanda, and I walked the building. Pete labeled the electrical outlets on his plans. We discussed the computer lab, stairwell addition, Child Care Center, air conditioning units. The building plans were submitted to the City of Colton. I will know the outcome on Monday, April 17, 2000. I spoke with Joe Lacko, he sounded hopeful about the transition on the building. The Corporation has to release the property or alternative financing will be sought. Mike and Joe are looking into alternatives – just in case.

I expect a positive outcome. The prophecy said 21 days from March 25th, it would be over. April 14th will be the 21st day. Today, I mailed the proof of Stephen Byabashaji's attendance to the African Summit in Washington to the Economical Employment Department. He outright lied on his mother's health. I am thankful that she is not in a coma. Jean Stevenson has completed the module I rewrote. She has done an excellent job. The consultant will have it by Wednesday.

Lord, guide us, bless us with a new home, students, and happiness.

4/11/2000 ~ 9:54 a.m.

Oh, He sent me messages of faith. Calvin Petty has stated his support to the Academy. He will 'make sure we are treated right.' Six students are enrolled into the CNA Program due to the urgency of need to have a class. The intake process has not been completed by the City JTPA Office. Calvin brought a student to class who has not received her admission pass. I was so grateful to him for his support. While I was on the computer working, I received a call from David, the photographer. He informed me of a trip to Africa Ghana in August. Before I could receive clear details, I received notice that Percy Harper was in the lobby. God sent Percy to me. He had been to the Beaver Medical Clinic. As he was heading to the freeway, the Lord told him to stop and deliver a message. The message was to "stay faithful, to seek Him. He hadn't given me 'this' to take it away. No one could do that, but Him. God has already worked things out. Fret not." As I began to share my thoughts of what had happened, Percy said, "No. The Lord has control." My communication must go up. I needed to spend time daily in prayer, in the Word, with the Lord. All my focus could not and should not be on the school. I had to STOP and spend time with God. In prayer – praising Him. I sat and listened to my friend of old. My friend, the Pastor, the message from God. He delivered the message and left, no goodbyes and hugs. He left the message and left as quietly as he had come in. I sat for a moment pondering his words. They were true. That I knew. I rose to say goodbye, catch him at the door. He was gone. STOP and pray. Stay in control with God. No anxiety, no fear, no tears. He sees all, knows all, and controls all. The building, Four-D Success Academy's new home. No obstacles that my Lord can't move. No finances that He can't generate. It is done. All is well with my Lord. As I arrived home, I knew I had to follow the day's message. In my room, I kneeled to give reverence to God. I prayed to my Father in Heaven. He heals me.

Lord, thank You, thank You.

4/12/2000 ~ 11:00 p.m.

God is. The property is released. Joe Lacko came to an agreement with Safeco. They signed the papers. Joe said $30,000 to complete the transaction. Mike called me, he asked if I was sitting down. Then he told me the good news. A big smile came to my face. I said to Mike, "Payday". He would finally get paid after two years, 6% of $1.6 million – about $96,000. I will call Joe tomorrow and give my thanks for his quick response to my call for help. The last line adjustment and family connection must be finalized. I thank God for all He has done. I thank God for the messages, for Percy's visit. I called Ernell first to share the good news; then I called Otis and the contractor. We were happy to hear the good news. Now he can assemble his crew. I informed Jean Stevenson and Charlie Seymour. I sit and think of God's goodness. I waited on the Lord, He fought all battles, and I sought no revenge. I prayed for the hedge of protection. I prayed for wisdom, I prayed for internal peace. I prayed for the students. I prayed for the faculty and staff. I prayed for the furniture to come. I prayed to stay focused. I prayed, I prayed. God heard my cry. He answered my prayers. I kneeled at my bedside to give thanks to my Lord. I see the school. I pray for the students who come with desire, thirst, and motivation to learn. I pray for staff that love the Lord. I see the OPEN HOUSE, the dedication of the Library to Neil Goodman, the dedication to my mother. Her picture hung in the lobby with words of love and appreciation for her financial support. It is all good. Sat/Sun the school will be represented at the Orange Blossom Fair in Riverside. We will recruit students for all programs.

Goodnight, Lord.

Friday is the 14th – the 21st day. Hallelujah.

The prophecy came true!

Today, the Vocational Nurse Board approved FDSA, the start of 45 students for 4/17/2000. Joe Lacko and I talked yesterday. I had called to give my gratitude to his efforts to aid the school. He acknowledged we had a signed contract and he would do what was necessary to make it right. He did. We have the opportunity to proceed with goodness for the students and faculty of the school. God has provided us His protection. Percy Harper shared/counseled me yesterday on God's promise, blessing, and our role in maintaining faith and obedience. I am so very blessed to have another day to make a difference in someone's life. One more day to thank God.

Lord, thank You.

The journey home will be filled with prayer and thoughts of His goodness.

6:15 p.m.

Same day. The journey home. As I sat in my seat on the bus, I gazed out of the window looking at the clouds. I have not jumped for joy. I prayed silently to God. I thought of much to do. Focus on the new home for the school. How do I thank Jean Stevenson for her devoted work? She has done an excellent job in improving the VN Program.

Four-D Success Academy, Inc. has gone through much in the last 12 months. I can't help but think of the focus of those who have gone, the anger, pain, and evilness that they take with them. What has been their reward? God's property will not be harmed. Four-D Success Academy, Inc. is God's property. God is. He has been my joy in my sorrow, the hand that designed my team, my foundation. The covenant with the Lord is unbreakable.

4/14/2000 ~ 11:39 p.m.

I kneel and pray, giving thanks to God. I thank God for the many prayer warriors He sent my way. This past year has proved to be a faith journey for me. I am firmer, faithful in process, and determined to do what God has planned for my life. He has allowed me to move beyond my wildest imagination. I, Linda L. Russ Smith, have the opportunity to be a business owner and owner with my husband of a $1.6 million building. We are blessed. As I prayed, I began to think of my father, Walter Russ, Sr. He died 5 years ago; I gained 10 pounds within a month. Over the past years since his death, I began to wonder what I would look like if I weighed 200 lbs. I believe I am near it, but as I prayed, I began to ask God to strengthen me to lose the weight, to remove. The desire to overeat, eat sweets. I prayed to weight 140 lbs. and wear a size 8 by August 7, 2000. The day I turn 48. Yes, I want to wear a size 8 for my 48th Birthday. All things are possible for those who trust in the Lord. 8 by 48. Lord, thank You for all. Love, Linda

4/16/00 ~ 7:47 p.m.

Oh, what a day. Day 2 at the Riverside Orange Blossom. Priscilla Brown, Registrar, and I. Recruiting for Four-D Success Academy. Yesterday, we were with a canopy and table. I had taken 2 chairs and a card table. The sun was warm, hundreds of people passed by. Our canopy and tables, chairs had been taken by another vendor before we arrived.

So... Today we arrived at 8-8:15 a.m. and transferred the canopy from the Amphitheater Center to our spot with the help of a gentleman passing through the grounds.

Robert Zamora stopped by. He has truly come to our aid. He gave us a $2500 spot for $800, free advertisement in the Tri Colored Brochure. 3-4 verbal ads from the stage. We had a very good response. By the end of the day, we were ready to hold the raffle. At 4:00 p.m. the day had been long, the outcome great. We were tired and the T.V. had to go. Priscilla, Alicia, Kathy H., and I recruited. Today, a lady walked by, saw the name on my jacket, the banner behind me and said, "Linda Smith, I have been dying to meet you." She had received the proposal I had written and submitted it to JTPA. She indicated it was the most detailed proposal she had ever reviewed. She had given it extremely high marks. I laughed with joy and gave her a hug. I told her I hope she was right. We were denied a contract last year. Her news was great. I then informed her I was preparing to write the Charitable Choice Proposal due Friday. She said she would be on the lookout for it. The Lord keeps blessing Four-D Success.

As I sit here writing, there is a song floating through my mind: *I expect a miracle. Believe it, receive it. I expect God to watch over us.* My heart is full, my body is tired. Tomorrow, we will have our class of VN students. Lord, thank You oh so very much, so very much.

I sit still – letting the words of the gospel seep into my heart and mind. I know God is with the school and me. The song, *'Lord, what shall I do? I am going to wait for an answer from You. I know that You will come through with an answer for me.'* Thank You.

4/17/2000 ~ 9:38 p.m.

BREAKTHROUGH

Breakthrough, God's blessings – Today the Class 12 of VN students started with 32 students. As I entered the room, I felt a sense of peace. Mr. Teo was speaking with the class, followed by Ms. Stevenson. Then Mr. Teo read his book of wisdom and said a prayer. I grinned as I thanked God for His blessing. This moment. We had survived. We stood as a unit against the test of tides, the odds of man, and are victorious with God. The class met Ms. Hansen, Ms. Sublim, and Ms. Brothers. We spoke words of encouragement, expectation, being on time. I told the class they were starting with an "A." Mr. Teo said an A+. Their goal is to maintain the A grade and have perfect attendance in 30 days. I took 20 books (Sadiq's) to Ms. Judy White. Tomorrow the Principals are having their meeting. Dr. Duneen DeBruhl will represent the book. I pray for an excellent response. If all the principals ordered a minimum of 100 books = $34,000 at $10 each. A start. It would be a goal to have 10,000 ordered. My mind drifts to the wonders of success. What would it be like to publish 70,000 books? Possible? Yes. As I leave the school, I decide to stop by A&P for a bottle of juice. I have a 4:00 p.m. appointment with the City of Colton Planning Department. Upon exiting the store, a young man informed me of the left rear flat tire. Satan never quits. He may not have put the metal into the tire – but he aids negative situations. I refuse to be overcome. Its 3:30, raining, and I have a flat tire. God, I will remain calm. I will make that appointment. A second kind man attempts to put tire sealant into the flat tire – it did not work. The hole is too big. I get the attention of a third young man. He aids this damsel in distress. He changes the tire. Rain pouring, I stand under the umbrella, unable to cover him. The more I tried, puddles of rain would roll from the top of the umbrella. I moved out of the way. By 4:00 p.m., Tracy was done.

He's a security patrol guard for a Middle School in Colton. I asked how I could pay him. He said, "I need a job. This one is for nine months." I laughed, he was serious. I explained my situation. I was moving and the staff and I had discussed the need for a security guard. We will be holding class in the evening and on weekends. I gave Tracy my card and told him to call me next week.

The members of the review team were concerned about the stairwell. Was it set back far enough? As I listened to the discussion, I began to pray and call on Jesus. I prayed for favor of the group. I needed the letter of approval. I was told to pick up the letter and pay the fee of $1,200 tomorrow a.m. They opened at 7:30 a.m. Ken Smith must resubmit drawings with the stairwell in a different position. Tired and overwhelmed with the last two hours, I pulled over to the side of the road to dry my eyes. I told myself there is nothing to cry about. I shouldn't feel overwhelmed, just keep doing what I need to do. God is ahead of me. I called Mike, left a message. I called Eugene. Home now, in bed. I prayed, I will rise to a new day with new opportunity to do good.

Lord, thank You. I call my husband to bed. Goodnight, Jesus, thank You for this day. I spoke with Yolanda. She reminds me everything is going to be just fine. Everything will work out in God's plan.

I look forward to the new day.

4/18/2000 ~ 7:00 a.m.

I awakened with scripture in my mouth. I was uttering Psalms – The Lord is my Shepherd, I shall not want. In my spirit, the Lord speaks,

"Fret not, for this day is mine. You are mine. All is well." This day is blessed with good news. Thank You.

10:54 p.m.

My good news is this – 8:30 Chamber Meeting at Colton, 9:00 a.m. Planning Department. I obtained the letter of approval for the extended structure and notice that the Planning Commission will give full note on May 8th at 6:30. The engineering supervisor gave verbal approval for the contractor, Otis, to start demolition. He provided his number for Otis to call. 9:30 the Department of Works searched for the Line of Adjustment. I am told the report would be in today.

At 10:00, I placed a call to Chicago Title to request the title report, maps, and address of local tenants. My plan is heard. 3:00 the call came from the Department of Works. The Lot Line adjustment is in. Before I could leave to pick it up, I received the call from Tammy. The maps, title report, and address are ready.

3:30 Students (3) come with a signed petition from class 11 to have a pinning ceremony. I think I surprised them. I was in total agreement. I shook their hands and told them I would pass it on to Ms. Stevenson.

At 4:00, I picked up the Lot Line Adjustment. I was ecstatic. I drove to Chicago Title Company. Tammy handed me the title report, labels, and map. I hugged her with joy – six-hour turn around – this normally takes 2-3 days. I also went to the County Building to record the Lot Line Adjustment. They wanted to charge $1.25-$1.75 per sheet to copy each sheet. I left and went to a private business. Copied the forms – 14 pages for $1.00, not $20.00. The County building was closed. So tomorrow, I will continue the blessing.

Jean Stevenson received a call from Jean Templeman and Ann Shuman. As I listened to the conversation, I took notes. It continues to be obvious Jean T. does not review the report in depth. She is so busy seeking fault. I became so angry. I sat in silence. I prayed for her removal. I asked God to silence her. I sat and listened to my anger. I asked for forgiveness, forgiveness for what I expressed.

God will protect the VN Program. Jean Stevenson is determined to be successful. I know the Lord is with us. Satan is very upset. We continue to bond in prayer. I rejoice in knowing Him – in seeing His wondrous works. We press on to the future. Stay focused, expect the best. From the best – God! As excited as I am, I hold much in me. I don't want to share all my joy until I have signed and handed over the $200,000 needed to close the deal.

The Lord will take care of it all.

4/19/00 ~ 6:58 a.m.

On Monday, Darlene returned to school. She came into my office to thank me and Ms. Stevenson for our action to dismiss her from the program. She thanked us for being firm in our decision, for insisting that she produces what was expected to be successful. She had a glow on her that was obvious. She shared the blessing God had placed upon her. She was a changed person. God had shown her the path. I pray she stays on it. She smiled a beautiful wide smile. She was changed. Lord, thank You for Darlene. Thank You for Four-D Success Academy. Thank You for allowing us to touch someone else's life in a good way. Thank You, thank You. My heart is light. You blessed me so as I sat and looked into the eyes and smiling face of Your saved child. Thank You, Lord.

Today, I will have continued blessing. Students will be lifted with prayer. Goals will be touched and saved. I kneeled and prayed to my Lord. He answers prayers. Thank You, Jesus.

4/19/00 ~ 11:02 p.m.

The end of another blessed day. Appointments one after another.

8:05 a.m. I met with Ken Smith and Pete. I provided the Lot Line Adjustment, map, addresses, and title report. This will aid in the presentation to the City of Colton Planning Department tomorrow. 9:00 a.m. I arrived at the City of Colton Planning Office. While traveling the 10 East, I contemplated if I should head straight to the County Building Office or go see Martin. I headed to see Martin. Glad I did. The submitted plans were on a shelf with a dozen or more other building plans. He had to search for FDSA's. Once located, Martin removed them from the pack. I inquired how long it would take to review them. Ken would be calling later in the day. He wanted an idea of any major changes that were needed. Martin agreed to the respective divisions for approval. Lord, I am glad I stopped by. The squeaky wheel gets the oil. I have been squeaking. Satisfied, I head to the next appointment with the County Records.

9:45 a.m. I headed to the County Records to record the Lot Line Adjustment. I paid the fee and headed to the bank.

10:15 a.m. I arrived at Business Bank of California to deliver the Lot Line Adjustment and the letter of approval for the T.I. Eugene and Jan were ready. I handed over the papers and Eugene was ready for me to sign the 1st set of papers. The loan is for $1,412,000. The T.I. $200,000 plus my $200,000= $1,800,000. The appraisal came in at $1,900,000. As we sign off the papers and discuss the content, Eugene notices my date of birth is the same as his. He was born

8/7/60. We laugh – we are good people. After signing the 1st set of papers, he informs me Ernell will sign in the appropriate section and the final escrow papers would be signed between Monday and Wednesday of next week. I felt great walking out of the bank. The school would have a permanent home! I can't wait.

At 11:10 a.m. I started to go to the office, but instead of going to the freeway, I think of Mr. Booker and the commercial. He was to deliver it 3 working days ago. My 1st judgment tells me to go see him. Good decision. He has the tape done. I requested changes. We reviewed old footage from the tape, selected the best shots. I will wait for a remake. I leave, heading to say thank you to Al Twine.

11:45 Al Twine has been a good friend and aid to the progress of FDSA in getting assistance to cross some barriers. I had to personally thank him for the plug with Colton City. He informed me that he had talked to Joe Rodriguez. Joe made the contact with Colton, and we moved forward.

12:45 p.m. I stopped to say hello to Attorney Otis Jones. Planned lunch for the next day. I headed to lunch, then to the office. We move forward.

Lord, thank You.

4/21/2000 ~ 11:45 p.m.

Yesterday, there was continued discussion between Joe Lacko and the company who originally purchased the property. Joe had to convince them that the Lot Line Adjustment would not decrease the size of the land they would own. They were not aware of the line adjustment and Joe had to finalize this last detail. Today, Mike Ballard informed me the demand for escrow would be issued on Monday or

Tuesday. Ernell and I could sign for the property by Wednesday or Thursday. As I heard those words, I remained calm. I was happy for Mike. After two years, a deal was about to close. I held my joy. I must sign them. I will rejoice. Oh I have been joyful each step of the way. I have witnessed God's miracles of finances, of change, of growth, of sustainment. He has kept us. I am joyful in knowing His works. My mind flowed with glimpses of what God has done in the last nine years. I shook my head. Oh, how He has used me. Thank You, Jesus!

Today, Ernell came to the office with the truck. He, Donnie, and Mike moved a sink and 4 tables to our storage. We truly are preparing for the move.

Students in class 10 left a note on my desk earlier this week. The message was to meet them alone behind the computer lab on May 26th at 8:30 a.m. I thought maybe they wanted to jump me now and try to beat me up. Now, I got God. I looked at the calendar – that's more than a month from now. I can wait.

We had a potluck today. There was plenty of good food. The office closed at 12 noon. But eight members were at the office at 3:00 p.m. I left at 4:00 p.m. Betty and Mary were working. We are blessed. We gave praises to the Lord. I said 8 at 48. But the way that cake and pudding went down, I may hit a roadblock if I don't tighten my lips. Lord, strengthen me to eat more nutritious foods.

Home at 5:00 p.m. Ernell left to attend his ski club meeting. Home alone, in silence, I kneel to pray. I give reverence to God. I praise His name. I am still to feel the peace within. I am still to breathe, relax, to feel. I am still for He is within. I give reverence to I AM. Thank You for this blessed day.

4/22/2000 ~ 11:35 p.m.

A lazy day. I awakened at 7:00 a.m. Too early to get up on a Saturday after the week I had. I dozed, watched the TV, listened to gospel, the Word, and dozed. I rose at 9:15. It had been raining. I decided I was going to stay in the house all day. Sweats on – comfortable. TV, food, wash a load or two, review some home assignments. I watched the clock tick away. I watched TV, Gospel Award Show, I prayed. Ernell and Aisha were out part of the day. My house was quiet. No one called for me.

The drapes open, light beaming through the glass panes, I relaxed. I thought of my life, the school, where we are, the finances. Let God. God has a plan. I relaxed the day away.

I need to think 8 by 48 more strongly. Having cake in the house is not good. Potluck yesterday, cake today, food at Momma's tomorrow. 8 by 48. Lord, cut my appetite. I need to lose weight. I pray for motivation. I need it.

Tomorrow, my family and I will be together.

I received a call from Zachary Russ. He has been to court and will return on May 12th. He will take the plea bargain if offered. I pray he gets sent to a halfway house. I became angry over the destruction of their lives and the depiction of the family. I pray. Lord, bless us all.

4/23/2000 ~ 11:49 p.m.

The end of Resurrection Day. The Lord sacrificed His life for me. Today, I attended Loveland Church with Ernell and Aisha. We had a blessed time in the Lord. I reflected that a year has passed. A year of pain, sorrow. A year of faith, growth, trust, and love. A year of survival. We have pressed through the breakthrough. As I sit still, I think of the financial needs for the next 4-6 months. God has the funds. He will guide us as a team to collect.

The loan on the escrow for 1020 E Washington, Colton will close by Thursday the 27th. What a day that will be. Oh what a day. A new home for Four-D Success Academy, Inc. I give praise and thanks to my Heavenly Father. Thank You.

Love, Your Precious Child

Faith has brought me through. Linda Lee Russ Smith

4/24/2000 ~ 10:28 p.m.

The call came today from Jay Smith of Business Bank of California. The papers are ready to be signed tomorrow. Ernell and I have an 11:00 a.m. appointment. When I heard the request, I sat quietly, unable to speak. Then all I could say was. "I will hold my joy until tomorrow. I must sign first." I am excited. This will be a historical event. I wonder how many African-Americans own a building in San Bernardino or Colton. Has God blessed me so? I sit and think I need pictures of this blessed moment. 'The signing.' I told Ernell we need to take the camera. He looked puzzled. I explained the reason. He agreed. Take the camera. Oh, I know, multi-million dollar deals are signed every minute of the day, but not with me. This is my first. It will not be my last. I plant a new seed.

I prayed to God to anoint the building with His blessing. Cover each and every person who walks through the door with His blood. The All State, Family Clinic, Child Care and School. That the spirit of Jesus abounds. That negativity is left at the door. I pray for abundance in students, abundance in revenue, to provide retirement benefits to the employees, supplies, equipment, educational support to faculty and staff, stability, and revenue to report. Ernell and I raised the

$80,000 within 12 months. I prayed for the hedge of protection, the angel's feathered wings, the words of God, His love. I prayed for wisdom, truth, love, and peace. I prayed for the rock to be my stabilizer in difficult times. I prayed for continued humility. I do all things though Jesus Christ who strengthens me. I pray for my gratitude to Jesus.

Lord, thank You.

4/25/2000

Ernell and I signed the papers.

11:00 a.m. appointment to sign loan application with Business Bank of California. As we were signing, I mentioned to Eugene Gonzales, VP Loans, that I wanted pictures of this historical moment. Ernell did not bring the right camera. Eugene informed me they (the bank) had a camera. He left the office and returned with an instamatic. Two pictures were taken of Ernell and me signing the documents. I am so excited. God has brought the school so far. In 1997, I could not obtain a $50,000 loan from any lending institution, including Business Bank of California. Today, I signed for $1,650,000. I think Ernell and I may be the only African-Americans who own such a building. Eugene informed me that the bank is going to submit my name for the SBA Entrepreneur of the Year Award for all counties. They feel I have a good chance to win. This is awesome. I sit in amazement. Our efforts may be recognized. All I did was trust in the Lord. My faith carried us through. In December, we did not have the $200,000, but I knew God had endless funds. The $200,000 would be in the account by the close of escrow. Even in February, when we were denied a VN Class, I knew the Lord would see us through. He did.

Jean Stevenson stood at the window holding a letter, smiling wide. As I slowly read the letter word for word, I became aware that God had answered our prayers. The letter informed us we would be assigned another consultant as of May 1, 2000. Hallelujah, Jesus! Jean Templeman was being removed as our consultant. The word spread throughout the building. Rejoice, for God is good – all the time! As I saw the mail, I noticed the grey paper. This is San Bernardino County. The word "Congratulations" hit me. My Lord, this is the answer to the last proposal I wrote. We passed phase 1. The letter gave instructions to complete the enclosed forms. They are due by Thursday the 27th. My Lord, this is wonderful. We lost the contract for the 1999-2000 year. We are being reestablished 2000-2001. The lady at the Orange Blossom had said it was one of the best proposals she had read. My God. I will prepare the paper and submit them by the end of the day tomorrow. I know the Lord will bless us with clients. Our new home is right on time.

I received a call from Stephanie at South Bay PIC (Private Industry Council). The contract is signed for the VN Program. Ernell will submit a new insurance form. Press forward. Months of word end in positive results.

Priscilla has composed a letter to mail to 80 Vocational Rehab Counselors. I know we will have positive responses.

I spoke with Dr. Duneen. The outcome of her presentation to the principals was extremely positive. The principals were very interested; one indicated he would order 1,000 books, books for every student in his school in Vermont. She expects many will order for the Fall. Lord, let there be no limit on the orders. What will come far exceeds my limited expectation.

Otis, Lacy, and I met at 7:45 p.m. We discussed the construction process. He signed bank papers. We are ready. He and his crew have their work cut out for them. June 7th we will be in a new home. The note will be about $3,500 more than our current payment. Lord, thank You.

Escrow will close between tomorrow and the 1st of May. My Lord is blessing us right now and tomorrow and for even more. I expect a blessing each day.

Lord, thank You so much. My heart is overwhelmed. Lord, thank You.

4/26/2000 ~ 11:46 p.m.

Today I worked on the San Bernardino County application. I had to do a little research to find some answers. I will complete it tomorrow for Mariana to type. We will turn it in on Monday. I received the escrow papers. The payment from Ernell/I and the school comes to $176,982.57. We have it. God just did His thing. We had nothing. I did not see it in December. We did not start a VN class in February. I knew God would do a miracle. Where else would the money come from? I will submit the final escrow papers to Chicago Title in San Bernardino, transfer the funds electronically, and turn in Otis Lacy's signed papers. Next Wednesday, May 3, Otis and the bidders will do a walkthrough at 1020 E Washington, Colton, CA 92324. June 7th is near.

Lord, keep us focused. We love You. Thank You.

4/27/00 ~ 4:03 p.m.

Today is the day escrow closes.

My Lord, my Lord, You did it. You guided me through the fog. That which I did not see, You saw for me. You brought us through. Faith has been my strong hold. Your words have comforted me. You said, "Fret not, trust me." Your words are the lamp unto my feet and the light unto my path. I am in awe of Your wonderfulness. You took nothing (of me) and made something (of me). Chosen by prayer, You called me by name on July 31, 1991 at 1:05 a.m. to rise and begin a new life, a life of devotion to You, a life of dedication to Your purpose for me and my life. Your love for me and my acknowledgment of that love has enabled me to serve others with a love and dedication only You truly understand.

For being a faithful servant, You blessed me and Ernell with a building valued at $1,900,000. Today at 11:00 a.m., I transferred $176,982.57 into Union Bank to close escrow. We purchased 1020 E Washington Street, Colton, CA 92324.

No person(s) who form weapons against Four-D Success Academy, Inc. shall prosper. God's the owner of it all. After delivering the signed escrow papers to Chicago Title, I called my mother, Eula Russ. The excitement in my voice told me and her of my joy. I told Momma that I would take her to see the building next week. She is excited for me.

Lord, thank You for her and her gift to the school in our time of need. We continued to stand. Momma, thank you. Monday, I will pass the notice to the staff and students of the new school's address.

My Lord, thank You for the gift. A home for Four-D Success Academy, Inc.

This has been a day of work. Here at Mammoth's Lake Sierra Lodge, I rose after Ernell left to ski. Listening to Gospel and reading *Success God's Way*, I relaxed. I prayed, then the telephone was needed. I called Lawrence Hampton Pal Centre. The VN students, who had not received/delivered their GED to Admissions, must complete the GED Program. Lawrence will research and then he and Jean will coordinate the needs for the students. We will get through this hurdle.

I had one last paper to sign to close escrow. The bank was concerned that the money was transferred on 4/27/00 and I was paying interest on the money without owning the building. After 6-10 calls between Century 21, Chicago Title, and Joe Lacko, the paper was signed and faxed to close. At 4:00 p.m., the Deed of Trust was recorded. Ernell and Linda Smith legally and officially became the owners of 1020 Washington, Colton. Mike and I stayed on the relocation project for two years. Lord, thank You for blessing us both.

4/29/00 ~ 12:36 p.m.

Today, I took a walk through the Inyo Forest National Park. It was a 1½ mile walk. The peacefulness surrounded me. I walked, singing from my heart, *Lead me, guide me.* The words flowed from my soul. Mouth opened wide, head tilted back, my heart opened to the joy of God's presence. I sang the song I sing when I need guidance. Today, I sang because God has led me through so many unforgettable storms. He has brought me out of many valleys. I sang unto the Lord. He has led Four-D Success Academy. As I walk the path I see to where my God is taking me, I am moved at His awesomeness. He chose one to do this work. I can only sing to Him. The forest is quiet as the song resonated about me. My Lord, thank You. I think of the past year. I have only come this far by God's grace and mercy. I walked and walked. I stopped, silence. I faced east, the sun. It cascaded through the tall pine trees. I lifted my hands up to receive the Lord. I submitted my prayers of thanksgiving. I prayed unto the Lord for His generosity, His love, for allowing me to forgive and for being forgiven. I prayed for the students, faculty, staff, furniture, the new building, and equipment. I prayed for my family, and for the Young Women Conference. I prayed to God to bless Four-D to provide $10,000-$20,000 to the God's Women Conference. As I submitted my prayer, I was overwhelmed by God's presence. He has granted me so much. I had to pray to purchase the building, but I think I realized that I needed to pray for a financial blessing to support GWC with $10,000. I know that God's blessing of $10,000 for August meant He had blessed the school to survive past June, and that the school would be reestablished. God would grant us this blessing and He would grant GWC with the blessing that I had put in my heart with a prayer. I believe my Father has endless funds. My God is my banker. He will provide. I claim what He has purposed in my heart.

Thank You, Lord, for the ability to give unselfishly. Your love for me cannot be equally met by me to others.

4/30/2000 ~ 11:01 p.m.

We arrived at home around 3:30 p.m., greeted by Aisha. It was good to be home. Relaxed for an hour or so, then Aisha and I went for a long walk. We covered about 4.5 miles. Halfway, we took the pilgrimage up Mountain Ave to Renee Webb's home. I was very tired. I had only been to her home once. If I had knocked on the wrong door, I still would have asked for water. We knocked on the right door.

After a short visit with Renee and her mother, Ms. Hall, Aisha, and I began the trip home.

Once home, we were greeted by Ernell. He said he was going to look for us. We were gone so long. I had called from Renee's and he thought I would want a ride home. He is thoughtful of me. I can't help but love him.

I called Donna and she shared the blessed news of the building. She was happy for me. We will get together this week for dinner.

Sitting here, I think of God's goodness. Tomorrow will be a blessed day. Thank You, Lord.

5/2/2000 ~ 7:28 a.m.

El Shaddai – He is more than enough. Planting seed- Creflo Dollar teaching. I think to myself, *What seed have I planted as he teaches on Christianity, and helping our neighbor?* Your neighbor can't pay their rent. You want to pray for them, but God has blessed you with more than enough. Your rent is paid, your bills are paid, and you have $500 left. Help your neighbor. That's the Christian thing to do.

I reflected on the male student at Riverside. His mother was confined to a wheelchair. Hot during the summer, she would sit in front of the cooling fan. Her son was behind on their rent by 3 months, he couldn't pay the utilities. He was a student in Four-D Success Academy Certified Nurse Program. He was trying to improve his life and his mother's life.

Once hearing of his plight, even his classmates were bringing food for his lunch. I contacted the landlord and utility company. I obtained the amount he owed and paid the sums, a donation from Four-D Success Academy. I sit and think how blessed I am, how blessed Four-D Success Academy is to have so much and to give. We have planted seeds. God has blessed us and he will continue to bless us. God is El Shaddai – He is more than enough.

Today, this morning, I listened to the words of Faith. Believe. I inform Aisha I am ready to write my book. I have recorded since 1991. There are many stories to tell. The journey thus far has been tremendously awesome, the pieces of a great puzzle are continually coming together. What I see thus far is beautiful. A gift from God.

My faith has kept me. God has protected me.

Lord, thank You.

5/4/2000 ~ 11:36 p.m.

There is so much to do. I am tired but not weary. I stay after work until 9:00 p.m. The quiet times between 5-9 allows me to address things on my desk: mail, checks, develop to do list for tomorrow – I ended with three items. The plans for 1020 Washington will be submitted on Monday. The Commission meets on Wednesday. I had the utilities changed over into Ernell's and my name. I contacted a Pest Control Service. I am taking bids for cleaning services. I am seeking a maintenance person. The fire system and security system must be established. I will establish a 'moving team' to organize the move for June.

I had to attend the Unemployment appeal against Stephen Byabashaija. As he lied and evaded the questions of the judge, I sat in amazement. I abolished him for falsely using his mother's health as a means for financial gain.

I am sleepy and tired. Tomorrow I have an 8:30 or 9:00 a.m. meeting with bookkeeping. A meeting with Managers, a meeting with Financial Aid Consulting Services, along with 13 items.

Goodnight, Lord!

5/7/2000 ~ 1:54 p.m.

On my way to Church this morning, I began to think of all of God's blessings. I know that God has had His way in my life. I asked that He come into my life when I was a child of 8 years of age. He has been with me and I with Him ever since. Oh, the paths I have followed have not always been that which He chose, but I am grateful for forgiveness. I am grateful for His grace and mercy. I am grateful that He heard my cry. Lost, but found. I have been on the path He would have me to walk. My employment has been under Him for the past nine years, and all that I have I have received from God, all that is built through FDSA has been built by God. Anyone who thinks they "built" any part of Four-D Success Academy lacks the presence of God. All things have occurred by Him and through Him. When I begin to take credit, as others have tried to, for what God has done, He will take back what He has established and given in His name. In 1991 I prayed unto the Lord, my savior, Jesus Christ. I prayed that He use me to do good works. That whatever, whatever He would have me to do, I was ready to work. I have worked. I have trailed long hours, striving to achieve the vision God placed in my heart on July 31, 1991 at 1:05 a.m. I don't know when my work will be over. I pray never. I have a love for Four-D Success Academy that I can't explain. Maybe the love of the school is as the love God has for me. I am blessed.

5/8/2000 ~ 11:04 p.m.

Tomorrow, Colton Planning Commission will approve the construction plans for 1020 E. Washington. Ken Smith and I will attend the meeting at 6:30 p.m. – Colton Chamber.

I received written notice from San Bernardino County – May 15th at 9:00 a.m. I signed the contracts for the new fiscal year. The contracts to training SB County residents in all five programs were lost. Lord, I am grateful to have earned the contracts back. I was told by one of the reviewers that my proposal was one of the best she had ever read in depth and detailed. The South Bay Contract will be resumed. I have signed the notation. Ernell will submit the insurance to the City of Hawthorne. The contract should be completed by May 18th.

I will call Erick – Department of Ed in San Francisco to obtain verbal approval of the CNA/HHA Program. This is important for our 90/10 ratio. I have pursued this outcome for 8 months.

We are planning the move. The moving committee is organizing. We are excited. Demolition will take place by Friday. I am so excited. Our new campus. Lord, I can't wait. The journey has been just that, a documented journey. Blessed by God.

I will write a couple of grants this month for "Friends." One on breast cancer for info to low income. PBS and radio announcement. The other to the California Endowment for Education and Training. I have begun the process to seek information to develop a two-year college.

My Lord, thank You.

5/9/2000 ~ 10:31 p.m.

Today, I gave keys to Avendel. Lacy Construction started demolition. This evening the Colton City Planning Commissioners approved the plans for the external stairwell. Peter, the architect, informed me the two plans were submitted Monday to the Building Department with the appropriate approvals. Upon final approval in about one week, Otis will be able to pull the permits.

Tomorrow, Otis, Avendel, and I will discuss minor modifications to the building plan. Priscilla has voiced her concerns about the move. We must start packing. As I look around, I see how much there is for us to do. Lord, my Lord, thank You. Linda

5/11/2000 ~ 11:02 p.m.

Never let up/down on prayer and never think all is well in the world. When one omits the presence of the spirit in prayer, worldly circumstances appear real and threatening. I thought yesterday, *Don't stop the prayer power sessions. Don't think. Easy street is with the Lord. Don't think. It can be done with prayer, faith, focus, productive action.*

The Water/Waste Department called. The fees to be online are high. A fee the employee would not mention. As much discussion and questions, I was told a man here would talk with the boss on Monday. I waited, but not before I told him I was going in prayer. He was in agreement.

I attended Dr. Herb Fisher's, Superintendent of SB County, fundraiser, a warm reception. I was greeted warmly by Dr. Fisher. I was introduced to several guests of his. It is good to network and become acquainted with others.

Tomorrow, I will attend Senator Joe Baca's Educational Summit at Valley College with several staff members. Today, the VN students celebrated Nurse Week by presenting Cultural Day. Countries were represented in custom, music, dance, food, and lecture. It was a joyful time. Excellent participation with students and staff.

Lord, thank You.

5/12/2000 ~ 11:48 p.m.

I attended the Congressman Joe Baca's 7th Annual Educational Summit with several faculty members. I made contact with Mr. Ramos – US Department of Education Information System. I inquired how to obtain funds for training for Vocational schools. He informed me of funding coming down the pike to school districts. They will be required to collaborate with private schools. I spoke with Mr. Cortez – San Manuel Indian. I obtained information and a contact to have a meeting. I seek a partnership to train Native Americans for employment in health care courses. I will call next week for a meeting. The office is located down the street from my home in Claremont on Foothill and Harvard. I spoke with Congressman Joe Baca. I requested that he keep Vocational Schools in mind as he reports Educational Initiatives. He introduced me to Donell. He will inform me of an RFP for funding. I will call him next week. I spoke with Dr. Caberllo, President of Valley College. I informed her of my desire to create a bridge with the college for Four-D students. She gave a positive response and referred me to the Director of Curricular Development, Marian Martinez. I will call her next week for an appointment. The Summit was a good networking environment for me. I spoke to the Pro Tem Mayor of Colton, Betty Cook. She was aware of the Academy move. I complimented the city's Planning Department for their support. I had not heard from Joe

Lacko regarding the Family Connection move. After we spoke, he said he would call me back. That was at 3:30 p.m. As I was leaving the office at 5:15 p.m., the telephone rang. At first, I started not to answer it, and then I thought, *That's Joe.* I answered. It was him with excellent news. Family Connection would be out on Sunday. The contractors could demo the suite on Monday. We talked about the fire alarm system. The telephone lines required connecting it to the Fire Department and the cost is $46 a month.

Oh, what a blessed day. I am so happy I stayed spiritually centered all this week. Monday, the Water/Waste Department will provide good news and a low payable fee to me to maintain usage of the system. My Lord has already provided a way for us. I spoke with Trudy Smith of the San Bernardino County Behavior Department Real Estate. The lease with the Clinic is ready for signature. A two-year extension will be signed on Monday. God is good. I delivered flowers to my mother. She was not home. She will know I was there when she sees the flowers on the center of her bed. Then, I delivered flowers to Momma Vivian – my wonderful mother-in-law. Home at last with Ernell and Aisha. I relaxed, thinking about my day, thanked the Lord, and watched the basketball playoffs. Life is good. My day was productive. Lord, thank You for this blessed day. I pray that I do all that You would have me to do and that which I do is done to represent You. I give You glory and honor. Thank You so much.

5/15/2000 ~ 11:35 p.m.

Happy Mother's Day

Another blessed day. Aisha surprised me by playing Lulla Rookh. This recital piece is a great classic English poem written by Thomas Moore in 1817. This was the last recital piece Aisha did under the training of Ms. Williams. I had only heard her play a song once in the last 6 years. I was thrilled. As I stood at the top of the stairs, I listened with joy in my heart. Each key brought back sounds of joy. I gleamed at her progress, her memory. My heart laughed as I held my chest. My mind skipped, delighted, head nodding as each struck key released a portion of the melody it was responsible for. My, my, my, it was not in vain. Seven years of lessons, it all worked out. For me, my gift to her came back to me on this day – Lulla Rookh. I took Aisha, Momma, and the twins to dinner at the China Palace – Momma's choice. They ate, became quite full, and went back home. Betty and Yolanda stopped by. Hugs, kisses, we were on our way. Tahira sent Ernell and I on a Reggae Party Cruise. It was different. The guests had to cook their own hamburgers. I chose not to eat. Cooking in the cold breezy air on a grill with the open boat moving slowly down the harbor is not my cup of tea. I did enjoy the dancing with Ernell.

Now sleepy and tired, I prepare for another blessed day. I know God is blessing each day of my life and I am so thankful.

Goodnight, Lord.

5/16/2000 ~ 10:25 p.m.

Never think it is over. Mishap lurks in the near corner. I attended the appeal hearing on Matthew Elbert. He was surprised I showed up. The look said it all. Jeannie Brothers accompanied me. Cherry was with him. I sat and listened to false statements. The judge had me ask questions – not make statements. I was astounded at his comments, although it was not time wasted. I will not pursue. This case, the judge ruled in Matthew's favor. I wish him well. His wages from Cherry are not adequate to provide for his family.

I spoke with Erick at the Department of Education. The CNA Program (312 hours) will not be approved. Several (3) students did not attend class for 10 weeks. They completed in 9 weeks. Dismayed, I pray the 90/10 ratio is good. We were about $4,000 short last month.

God will provide. I think of the cost to move ($5,000-$6,000). The office furniture, telephone $7,000, roofing repairs $1,800, rent $12,980, utilities $500. Lord, get us through this. I seek a calm spirit. Keep pressing forward.

Keep us safe.

Financially secure.

5/17/2000 ~ 8:49 p.m.

God is working it out.

I sit, shaking my head while driving to work. I began to think of the Planning Discussion at Colton. I had not heard from Marty. Had any other plans been approved? As I drove, I thought, *He will call.* I passed the 9th exit. As I ascended the Mt. Vernon exit, the Spirit directed me onto Mt. Vernon, away from my office. I was heading towards the Planning Office. As I entered the Planning Office, Marty greeted me. He was working at a computer. In review, the list of approval he rated, one had not come in. He would follow up on it. He also was surprised that four weeks had passed since the initial approval. I inquired about the Water/Waste approval. Mary was aware that Rex was working on the approval for the school. I was given directions to the Colton Water/Waste Department on L Street.

Leaving the Planning Office, I began to debate in my spirit. Should I go? No, I should go to the office and call. No, there is nothing like a personal presentation. This is a good day. As I sat in the office speaking with Rex, I realized he was helping the Academy. He was lowering the fee greatly, according to the numbers presented. As we talked, my "load" lightened. The fee of $16,000 plus was dropping, dropping, dropping. At $3,020, we agreed that the amount was acceptable. Then we discussed "meter fees." The city codes required two meters. The building has one, or I could submit a letter to waive the 2nd meter and pay $0.88 per 760 gallons of water. Rex informed me it would take 29 or 39 years for $0.88 to pay for a new meter. I chose the letter. God is. Rex informed me he would prepare his report, review my letter, and submit it to planning for approval. He now only had 10 more to review. My Lord, thank You for sending me to Rex this day. A financial blessing and time saved. Lord, thank You.

I kneeled and prayed, thanking God for protection. I prayed for my family, brothers incarcerated, my mother, peace, her health. I thank God for forgiveness, love, peace, my marriage, His salvation, my children, protection, focus, Aisha- Impact Group Growth, her desires for life – her ministry growth. I prayed for Tahira's protection as she travels the bold path. I prayed for wisdom, her ability to make the right choice. I prayed for her path. I prayed for the school and its growth. I prayed for students: 45 in the upcoming VN class, 20 in the Pharmacy Tech, 20 in the Medical Billing. I prayed for unity in spirit among all staff. I prayed for the unspoken ethical rule – that no one ever speak negatively against another school. I prayed that God lifts us above all other, that our performance outweighs/outlives the negativity of others (schools). I prayed that FDSA students shine and rise above all. I prayed for Board to pass ratio success. I prayed for the new home of the school. I prayed for favor with the

Department of Education, the ABHES group. I prayed for wisdom and peace. I prayed to my Lord. I am so thankful for all that He has provided. His word is a testimony to that with God, all things are possible.

I can't say enough about what He has given me. I get overwhelmed with joy when students tell me of their success and employment. It is all worth it. I would do it over again. Lord, I am lucky. As I was told today by a man here, "You are doing a wonderful job to help others. That should make you feel good." It does. I sit in my high-back black chair and smile to myself. I am lucky. No, I am blessed and I know it.

I have visited the construction site three times. The view is different. I see the tracks for the wall frames. The classrooms will be good sizes. I am excited – a new home for Four-D Success Academy. We are blessed.

Lord, thank You.

5/20/2000 ~ 10:53 a.m.

It never ends. My spirit is stirring. I reached for the phone in my office. I had not heard from ABHES regarding the outcome of the last report submitted. I was told to call in my spirit. I spoke with India. She informed me the reviewer did not accept the Effectiveness Plan multiple question. I would probably receive a deferment. That I could not have. I had previously been deferred twice on two separate issues. I asked India to please share her comments with me. She did. She recommended I call Chris on Friday a.m. for advice. I did.

While speaking with Chris, I realized I had to respond before Monday with a new Effectiveness Plan. I requested his guidance. He responded. He referred me to page 37 of the ABHES regulations and to another school director who had visited the Academy – Ann. Hearing the tension and concern in my voice, Ann opened the door of understanding. She faxed me her Effectiveness Plan and gave me her home number. Ann Logan and I stayed at the office until 10:30 p.m. on Friday. Ann Logan compiled statistics while I began writing a new plan. I was exhausted when I arrived home at 11:00 p.m. Unable to hold a conversation with Aisha, she directed me to bed. 6:00 a.m. awakened relaxed. Rose at 6:25 to the computer in my office, I began to organize my thoughts. I began to write. I did quite a bit. By 10:15, I had to stop and prepare for my 12:00 presentation at the Echos of Faith Church in Ontario for a group of teens. While there, I met Kelly O'Connell of IESD. She is in favor of FDSA and has sent several students to us: Dr. Lovia, veterinarian, Milton and Yvette Butler. Milton is a Physician Assistant and Stock Broker. We had a good time laughing and talking about skiing and investments.

By 1:15 p.m., I was on the road to SB. I picked up my cousin Betty at Momma's and headed for the NCNW Membership Tea. We recruited new members and invited old members back. It was quite nice. We left the tea at 5:30 p.m. Back at Momma's, Betty and I chilled. We visited with Momma until 6:30. Then we headed to Dr. Will and Lana Robert's for an evening of bliss, jazz, and barbeque for a scholarship fundraiser and celebration of the African-American 1042 A Combat Battalion. We wrapped up the evening at 9:00 p.m., said goodbyes and thank you's. Betty is home. I was on the freeway heading west. Music low, car smooth, I relaxed. A full blessed day. Tomorrow, I will attend Church, praise God, seek and receive guidance to completing an acceptable Effectiveness Plan. I am in His will.

Ernell left yesterday to his annual River Rafting Trip. I know he is safe from harm. He is in the presence of God – His protection.

Lord, thank You for a blessed full day. Always, Your Child

5/21/2000 ~ 11:25 p.m.

Today, I rose at 6:25 a.m. I attended the 7:30 a.m. Church service. I could not miss Church. I had to go for the Word and for my blessing. Pastor Chuck spoke from Galatians 3:1-16. The spirit, the miracles, the gospel, what is the truth. I am thankful for the Word of God. His spirit, love, and gospel have been my protection and blessings. I am experiencing His miracles and blessings. I believe in the gospel. Jesus was born, crucified, died, rose, and is returning. Following Church, I drove to my office. I had to complete the ABHES report. But, before going there, I visited 1020 Washington. Pictures were taken of the construction in progress. The pictures will be great for the memories. At the office, I settled into my chair, turned on the computer and began writing. 11:30-8:30 I wrote, reviewed, made changes, called Ann Gibson, made copies, and figured out how to add page numbers copied to the main copier. By 8:30, I was done. I faxed a copy to Ann. She will call by 7:00 a.m. I prayed to God that what is written is acceptable by ABHES. I prayed for a 3-5 year approval.

I pray for a blessing.

5/22/2000 ~ 2:10 a.m.

Exhausted. This past weekend, I had a full schedule from Friday until yesterday at 4:00 p.m., I seemed to be in motion. The ABHES

Linda L. Smith

report was due Monday morning to Chris. I am so very blessed to have talked with Ann Gibson. Her input, guidance, and samples provided me with the foundation to write the Effectiveness Plan. I worked on the development of the plan for 4 hours on Friday and 9 hours on Sunday. On Monday morning, I received a call from Ann at 5:15 a.m. She had reviewed what I had written. She stated it was extremely well-written, two recommendations to add titles for clarity. I thanked her, made the changes, and faxed the report to ABHES by 6:00 a.m./9:00 a.m. Virginia time. I made several calls throughout the day to assure myself that Christopher Eaton had obtained it. He presented the report to the commissioners. I have prayed for a full clearance and an approval for a 5-year extension. Following the submission of the report, I prepared for the day's work. Tired and moving slowly, I thought of all the things I had to do. On my way to work, I was paged by May Helen at Otis Lacy's contracting services. The permits from the City of Colton cannot be pulled. The architect's final drawings are not in. I exited the 10 freeway at Euclid. Heading south, I arrived at Pete Veloba's office. It was 11:30 a.m. He was out. I waited. He arrived at 12:15. We discussed the requirements. Ken Smith called the Colton Planning office and spoke with Marty. The Plan changes are made. I left to take them to Colton. I received another page from May Helen. The tree where the stairs must be built must be removed. I called Ernell and Wendy. I needed help. The tree has to be out by today at 7:30 a.m. I receive a call from Otis. Vouchers for payment need signature. Heading north on Euclid, I passed the 10 E entrance and take the 10 W entrance. I drove to San Dimas. I signed vouchers, viewed plans, then headed out to Colton at 1:20 p.m. I arrived at Colton at 2:00 p.m. Marty received the plans and informed me the fee is about $5,000. He will review the plans and have the permits ready by 10:00 a.m. If

182

his office is slow, he will do the inspection Tuesday or Wednesday. I need it ASAP. My heart sank. I felt the emotions swelling within me. He must have seen the change in my face. He said he will try. I exited, feeling the tears swell up within me. I was tired. I then headed to the Colton Utility Department in City Hall. I have a Security Bond for Margie. This Bond of $350 prevented me from paying $3,500 to keep the utilities on at the building. Margie was out. I waited about 20 minutes. The bond was signed and witnessed. I left the office at 3:25 p.m. I placed calls to follow up on the tree. Wendy had someone. I called Ernell. We talked, and I expressed how tired I am. NCNW Board meeting tonight – he recommended I go home. The Board can make it without me this day. I took his advice. Home, I ate a big bowl of oatmeal and drank a glass of juice. Then, I was directed to bed to sleep by Aisha. I fought falling asleep, but by 4:45, I was out. I slept until 12:05 a.m. Now, here I am. Unable to return to sleep, I rose to pray. I pray for staff, those who are sick, family, and the students. I express gratitude to God for being so merciful for His grace. I pray for ABHES. I pray for continued support to work at FDSA. I pray for wisdom.

The Lord's blessings have been tremendous. Otis offered to carry ½ of the $12,000 to build the staircase for 3 weeks. That gives me time to raise the funds and only pay out $6,000 up front, a wonderful blessing.

It is 2:45 a.m. I will go back to sleep.

Lord, thank You.

5/23/2000 ~ 11:17 p.m.

Gratitude. Joyful. Moist eyes. Light hearted. Prayerful. Thankful. I clung to the approved plan. Marty had given the stamp of approval. It was happening. 1020 was being transformed into our new home. Now the contractors would be able to move ahead. June 7, 2000 is two weeks away. I hurried to the car and called Ernell. My voice resonated with good cheer. He was pleased for me. I delivered the plans to Avendel. He is ready for the plan check. The stair builder was present and working. Men were inside building walls. I could see it coming together. Offices, modules, and the receptionist area. Reality hits. I beamed with internal joy.

I signed a contract with Adelphia Cable to air our latest commercial. Laura brought the prices down to an appreciated level of $1,000 a month for 12 months, $250 a week for 40 spots. I have prayed for an overflow of blessings. I await the ABHES and the Board of Nursing report, but not without prayer. I have prayed for the hedge of protection, for favor from the reviewer and writers. My faith carries my thoughts. My strength comes from the Lord. All I can do is pray. And that is enough. Pray in faith and act according to the spiritual guidance. He knows all and is the provider.

Peace, be still. Lord, thank You.

5/24/2000 ~ 10:54 p.m.

Unable to sleep, I awakened at 4:00 a.m. Thinking of the new office, I wondered if the modular areas were wide enough. Was Wendy's space deep enough? My desk was over-stacked. Up at 4:45 a.m., I prepared for work. Dressed and out the door at 5:25 a.m. Said goodbye to Ernell. Received a mumble. I arrived at 1020 at 5:50 a.m. Entering the building, I heard sounds. Larry, the maintenance, was in the building. I walked, took measurements, reviewed the plans, and realized the receptionist area did not have a window; the assistant area lacked the testing table. The wall did not extend to the ceiling in the west hall. By 7:00 a.m., I had shared my findings with Larry. I stopped by Ms. Alice at 7:00 a.m. We laughed, talked, and praised the Lord for two hours. I spoke with Pumpkin (Alice). I received her resume for a possible job opening. At 9:00 a.m. I returned to 1020, reviewed findings with Avendel, and am now off to my office. Daily work, questions, little done on my desk.

Tonight, I will sleep until 6:00 a.m. The desk will be there in the a.m.

Lord, thank You.

5/28/2000 ~ 10:35 p.m.

Peace is within when I have done all that I can do, when I know I have done my best, when I know God provides, when I know I've stayed on the path. I know the power of I AM. I have peace. As I think and reflect on the journey, I often just shake my head. The testimony is so very powerful. I think of the naysayers, those who said, "They were going to close the school down." The words that the heads of other schools were going to run Four-D out of business. I think of limited to no funds six months ago. Today, I own with my husband a 30,000 square foot building for $1,600,000. I think of this tremendous testimony of God's giving, of my faith, of not giving up. This is truly a testimony. All thoughts crowd my mind. I don't question how it happened. I saw it unfold. Like sitting in a motion movie, I watched the scenes reveal the character in the play, plots unfolded. Cliffhangers resolved, truth unfolded, joy released. Tears flow, rejoicing happening. I am the witness to God's words, "Trust in me, fear not unto your own understanding."

Today, as Aisha and I enjoyed our walk along Mills St., she and I shared in our discussion on my desires for a new home. I told her I had all but given up on my dream home. She was quick to remind me of the power of prayer. I was reminded that I prayed for a new school. I was specific in my prayer. I prayed for 30,000 sq. ft., lots of parking, freeway access, a stand along building, close to restaurants, and a child care site. All I have. She spoke in details. The size of the house, single or two story, the lawn, the type of mailbox, income to support it, a view of the city lights, cul-de-sac or corner lot, the size of the garage, the color of the house, furniture, with or without a pool, and spa. Pray for the specifics. Pray like I prayed for FDSA. She was quick to tell me if I prayed for a home like I prayed for the school, I would already have the home I wanted. It is so important that I keep focus and that I receive all blessings from God. I never want greed to be a part of my life. I would love to have the house with white pillars, 4000 square foot, lap pool, spa, 4 bedrooms, den, office, 3.5 baths, and single floor with steps. A beautiful lawn, multiple color flowers, and lots of green bushes. Furniture that is elegant but simple, an exercise room, 3-car garage, and space for a boat. It is out there. God will provide. I will pray and trust. I am comfortable in Claremont. I want to stay in the city of Claremont. Envision the house, pray for each room. It is okay to want more. God is a God of abundance.

I asked. When the book is written, what will it be?

It is 11:15 p.m., time to retire for the night. Tomorrow is a new day of blessings for my family and me.

Lord, thank You.

Your Child, Linda

He is preparing us, taking us to another level. Today, I began to pack up my office – taking plaques, pictures, statues, and dolls. Wrapping each with newspaper to prevent damage during the move. As I handled each piece, I studied it. I read quickly over the words of recognition – the names on the dolls from the Home Health Aide Class of 1993, the lamp from the Magnificent Seven of Riverside. The letters from state and local legislate. The original document of July 31, 1999 at 1:05 p.m. The pictures of family members. I paused, holding the photo of my dad, and smiled proudly. We looked forward to the future. Physically absent in my life, I could feel the spirit of His presence. I thanked him for the encouragement, "Daddy, I am moving forward and God is with me." I gathered the pictures of my mom, the twins, Tahira and Aisha. Wrapping each and placing them in the box labeled, President CEO, color-coded purple. I will have a photo of Momma and me for my new office. I placed Virgil's cane in the box. It will have its own spot in my office. I cleared the walls and the top of the bookshelves. Sitting in my chair, I contemplated the future, looking at the past, conscious of the present. I sat quietly. Five years – April 8, 1995 to May 30, 2000. How time has gone by. Five years, now memories forever. The future is bright, filled with God's loving protection and omnipresence. Lea called about the old Campus Crusade Building. The owner is looking for a tenant. Sounds good, but I'm committed to Colton. I informed her of our upcoming move. She suggested I pray on it. The owner is willing to do T.I. rent at $30 sq. ft. – an extended site, a non-profit child care. God will lead me. We made payroll without using the line of credit. Thank God! I move forward with God. "There is no power that can separate me from God – none!" Jesus, thank You.

6/1/2000 ~ 7:51 a.m.

I'm too sad to write. Yesterday, Otis informed me that the move date of June 6th would probably not be met. There are delays with the carpet, survey approval, and painting. I was numb. The advertisement on the move is out, the sign is down, packing taking place. I had to sit still. Let God be God. The outcome is there. I just don't see it. This incident was my reminder to stay in prayer for all things. Comfort in life, in daily situations, should never exclude prayer.

Off to work to be blessed with God's miracles, love, blessing, and joy. Today is a good day.

Thank You, Lord.

6/1/2000 ~ 11:59 p.m.

It was a blessed day. I requested an extension from Linda Stratton until the 14th. Request denied. Otis had a contingency plan. Move items into the student lounge and the conference room. Paint and carpet finished, and we are in. But there's a possible small hold up. Ernie, the surveyor, informed Avendel that the drywall had to be re-hung, as a small gap was present. This would require removal of the wall, turning it and reattaching. Avendel and I met at the City office for help. We talked with Marty and Ernie. We got the approval from Marty to move forward. There we received recommendation for the commode installation. All went well. Arrangements in place for the telephone, computer lines, mail transfer, equip, and the sign removed from the current building. Tomorrow, we will continue to pack. Our last staff meeting held. I thanked the staff for 5 years of support. I thanked God for keeping us. We will move forward as a positive team guided by God. I am so thankful. 30 more days before the fiscal year end. Lord, grant us a financial positive end. Bring us through.

6/2/2000 ~ 11:24 p.m.

Packing up, I amused myself today. I prepared for the regular management meeting scheduled for 9:00 a.m. But, to my surprise, when I entered the office, Aja was wearing jeans, happily stating, "Ms. Smith, how do you like my packing jeans?" Wendy arrived in jeans. I realized I was the only one thinking of the meeting. I dare not say a word. I figured if I did they would have thought I was truly crazy. There was packing to do. Toni was in my office taping up a box. The refrigerator was being cleaned, kitchen items packed. Everything came off the walls. The excitement was in the air. Today, we selected the countertop. Tomorrow, Margie and I will select the tile.

Now – Aja has started 'Fight the Fat at Four-D'. We weighed in privately by Mary Salim. Mary was selected because everyone trusted her. I weighed in at 192 lbs. I will win the weigh-in money at the end of the month. I had wanted to see what I would look like at 200 lbs.—now I know. Now it is time to go back to 150 lbs. and my size 9-10. My goal is 8 at 48 by August.

Today was a blessed day.

I am now mentoring Tina. She did not do the assignment. No written report. Therefore, she was assigned to read a second story and write two reports by 12:00 noon. I'll see how she does.

Goodnight, Lord.

6/4/2000 ~ 11:28 p.m.

The testimony went forth at Loveland Church. Two weeks ago, I left a message on Pastor Chuck's phone. I requested to give my testimony.

So much had happened in 8 years, and this year was the blessing of the building.

I gave the testimony at the 7:30 and 10:00 a.m. services. I shared God's blessings: the $1,650,000 gift and the purpose of 'tithing'. I prayed that the spoken words of my mind would touch someone. They did. I thank the Lord for the opportunity to give my testimony.

I got a call from Walter Jr. – Momma was in the ER at Kaiser. She had fallen at Church, possible fractured arm. My spirit told me not to worry. Momma has strong bones. It may be a hairline fracture, but nothing serious. When I arrived, she was fine. A hairline of the humerus. While at Church, a young man recently released from jail sang a song. He reminded her of her three sons incarcerated and Harry Templeton. She said he is singing like Harry. She went out to the foyer, fell to her knees and face, overcome with emotions. Donnie was at Church with her and witnessed the fall. God protects her always. No head injury. Minor discomforts. God's spirit. CT scan negative. Lord, thank You.

Sleepy. Goodnight.

6/5/2000 ~ 11:33 p.m.

The pressure is relentless. I can't let up. Yesterday, I had the opportunity to give my testimony to the Loveland congregation. I was honored to share God's blessing and to lift others with hope. I visited the site. There is much to do. The painters did not work as planned on Sunday. This delay moved our moving plans around. Otis, Avendel, and I went to plan C. We will move the upper room furniture into the student lounge. Move the lower floor items into the Child Care Center. I expressed anger when Wendy said, "Donnie said the move will be delayed. They aren't ready." I have tried very hard to address keeping the staff morale up. I was approached by 3 staff about the move following Wendy's statement. This is how rumors spread to faculty, students, and the community. I wasn't given the opportunity to address this issue properly. I blew up. Wrong, yes – but there are times that I seem to constantly work on 'fires.' I do expect the managers to respond more appropriately.

ABHES wants more. I can't write about it now. I was just bewildered. More to write. The Bureau wants to see the building before I move but suggested I not sign the lease — mass confusion. More calls and writing. I pray that God relieves me one day of pressure. I want everything right. I want to develop the Child Care Center, more programs. All I can do is keep praying.

6/6/2000 ~ 7:30 a.m.

My mind is tossing with thoughts of the school: the ABHES outcome, the Default Program, the VN Program, the Placement Rate – how to thoroughly address each item. I awakened at 2:00 a.m., tossed at 3:30. Lying awake, I prayed to God for guidance. I made a note on a pad in the dark. Restless at 5:00 a.m., I rose. Entering the den, my heart was heavy and full. I kneeled to pray. I asked God for help. I almost couldn't pray, the words got stuck in my throat; my mind's thoughts caused pounding. I cried to relieve the pressure. I know God will bring us through this series of crises. I testified of His goodness and that has not ended. Sleep overcame me. This is a blessed day that the Lord has made and I am glad to be in it.

Lord, thank You.

6/6/2000 ~ 9:58 p.m.

A blessed day it was. Jean Templeman continues to be the wonderful thorn in the side. She recommended we enroll 20 students. Her

191

rationale – Jean Stevenson needs the assistance of the staff to write the new curricular. Jean was furious. She has submitted module 1, module 2 will be sent next week, and module 3 is due in October. God has a way of protecting us. We were not recommended for a non-start. 16 students are graduating in June. We will enroll 20-30 in July. Jean S. will request the Board allow a start of 30 students. The Bureau gave verbal approval to relocate. The letter I received was incorrect. The ABHES letter arrived yesterday. I will request to go before the Board in October/November. I will submit a written report.

The movers will arrive at 8:00 a.m. We will be ready. Margie and Wendy shopped for the receptionist area. They are truly involved in redecorating. Priscilla is doing the student lounge. Betty, Mary Salim, Charlie, and I held hands and prayed before we left this evening. Five years seemed like yesterday. Mary, Betty, and I, along with Margie, are the only original group members from the Foothill Claremont site. We have come a long way. God is good. From two students to 4,000. From myself to 38 employees. From 1,100 square feet to 30,000 square feet. From $798 a month to $1,650,000 ownership. God and only God has brought us this far. The future of Four-D Success Academy, Inc. is going to be so exciting. It will be something to watch unfold: more programs, more students, more staff, more from working for the Lord.

I am still asking the Lord to use me.

Thank You, Jesus.

6/8/2000 ~ 1:12 a.m.

THE MOVE.

We are in. I arrived at work on 6/7/2000 at 6:45 a.m. Aja was already there working and packing. The crew began to arrive at 8:00 a.m. The Allied moving van Services arrived at 10:00 a.m. This was an exciting day. As I entered into classroom 3, I began to cry, overcome with the emotions of moving on. We had come so far. From 1,100 sq. ft., 2 students, one staff person, 1 computer, 1 hospital bed, 3 desks, to 8,000 sq. ft., 32 staff members, 15-20 computers, furniture, and equipment in every room. Now 30,000 sq. ft. Space for more staff and an additional 35 computers, the Child Care Center, and tenants. Four-D Success Academy, Inc. was being blessed by God. The tears flowed; all I could do was thank God for His goodness. The movers worked until 11:45 p.m. That's when I locked up, lights off. I had a minor controversy with an employee of the clinic. Her approach and rudeness required I state my position on the health and safety of all. I do pray the business relationship remains pleasant.

Well, I must rise early. It is 1:30 a.m. Goodnight, Lord.

Thank You for a new home for the school.

6/9/2000 ~ 11:03 p.m.

We've come this far by faith. As I drove up to the campus, I was in awe of its greatness...God's greatness. It is beautiful. We have come so far. I have given little thought to 952 So Mt. Vernon Ave. It is behind us along with the unpleasant memories. I entered the building viewing the steady progress. Carpet going down on the second floor, new doors being hung, my office coming together with a private bathroom. The signs were decided on between Wendy, Margie, and I. The payphone is coming tomorrow.

We set up a makeshift office in one of the classrooms, so business was going on. Students have come by to pick up their gowns for graduations. Their comments have been very positive. God is blessing us. The staff (some) is off until Tuesday. All report to the school at 8:00 a.m. to set up the second floor.

We are blessed. We will end June 30th with a positive net!

Thank You, Lord.

6/11/2000 ~ 11:46 p.m.

I prayed for abundance financially. I prayed for students to overflow the class by July. I prayed for 10% increase to all staff and $10,000 to GWC. He will provide. I prayed for full range of motion to Momma's left shoulder – a complete healing. I prayed for Momma Julie and Momma Vivian's continued health. The Lord answers my prayers.

Tomorrow is a blessed day. The Lord will provide the financial blessing to GWC, and in doing so Four-D staff will be blessed.

All is all right with the Lord.

6/12/2000 ~ 9:55

Tired. Tired. Tired. We cleared out the student lounge. It was packed. We had more tables and chairs than I thought, enough for every classroom. All 13 beds, equipment, boxes upon boxes of items. Upon arrival, I notice the 2nd floor had not been cleaned as requested. I was given a lame excuse about the power going out at 1:00 a.m. I informed the service I would take care of it myself. I will change services in July, if not sooner. Windows, blinds, tables, and chairs were cleaned, dusted, bathroom mopped, Cloroxed, walls painted, stalls wiped down, and carpet vacuumed. Snack machines came in, three big ones. We worked. At the end of the day, I saw progress. As I looked down the long hall, every room was taken. I thought to myself, *We will outgrow this in five years.* I began to think of expanding into the 1st floor. Allstate suite, then the clinical area. In 5 years, we will need another building. The Orange Coast site is also 31,000 sq. ft. The Lord will prepare us. Well, Lord, we thank You for this blessed day. Goodnight.

6/19/00 ~ 11:00 p.m.

Today is Father's Day. I thought of my father and smiled. He is always with me. His words, his prayers, and his smile. Today while shopping for Ernell's gifts, I stopped to try on a pair of shoes. I needed an 8½ww. No go. Store only had an 8M. I thought of Daddy, his feet, my feet. I can't go far without him. I returned to my shopping spree for Ernell. Today, he was treated. He got 2 sports coats, 5 pairs of pants, 15 shirts, 10 ties, and two pairs of shoes. He was pleased.

Tomorrow, we move the first floor out. I can't wait to settle into my office. I spoke with Jean yesterday. The Board approved a class of 20 for July 17, 2000. After Jean heard that another school was denied a start for October, she made the wise decision not to request 30 students. We will make it. The enrollment has increased with the MB/HCE/Pharmacy Tech Class.

Lord, thank You for keeping me safe from everything.

6/25/00 ~ 7:00 a.m.

Yesterday, I attended the summer of 2000 Graduation held at Cal State San Bernardino. We had 80 students, 400-500 guests. Dr.

David Taylor was the guest speaker. I was moved to see the fruit of my efforts. C.J. graduated. I have always believed he was a special person with gifts to be a very good nurse, but during the course of study, he deviated. He was held back and had to report Module 3. His success delighted me. The outcome is as I knew it would be. He took responsibility for his actions and I held him accountable. He succeeded. He was proud at the ceremony. He assisted Priscilla Brown with organizing his classmates for the ceremony. He beamed. His family beamed. His father cried. His brothers took pictures with me. As I looked into the faces of the graduates, the guests, and our staff, I thanked God for the journey. I would do it all over again. Lord, thank You. A grateful person I am.

6/27/2000 ~ 8:30 a.m.

Food diet – Healthy body.

Ecclesiastics 10:17 and 5:17

Proverbs 22

Proverbs 14

Proverbs 5:23

Proverbs 19:23 4:20-22

Proverbs 29:10

Isaiah 5:11 Drink water

Ecclesiastics 3:13

I must lose weight. My energy is moderate. I have a ton of energy for the school, but all else is limited. I have gained weight these pass 3 days. I see it and feel it. Pastor Copeland's message today was on healing and having a healthy body.

I cleaned my house. I vacuumed the floors, washed, folded, put up all the clothes, changed linen, cleaned my office, cleaned the dining room table of my office items, and remembered the 10-year-old flowerpot. My house is better than it was yesterday.

Tahira took the stepper to her house. I will devote more energy to myself and my home.

Ernell called at 9:30 p.m. He is on his way home from the river. I have missed him. I know he and the fellas had a great time.

Tahira called this morning at about 9:40 a.m. She was very angry that she had been ordered to work a double. I explained to her that she was not on her path God has laid for her. She has been on someone else's path. She should have been in school or Church. She was tired, irritable, angry, and emotional. I told her to eat, drink some juice, dismiss her anger, and provide good patient care. I also explained to Tahira that she is my responsibility. As my child, I am responsible in advising her and keeping her on track toward her goals. I stressed she must complete the RN Program, stop working on Sundays, and focus. I stated my love and said goodbye with a request she call me later in the day to talk. Tahira called back within 4 hours. She felt better. She wanted me to know she had eaten, had juice, and had a few catnaps. She felt better. Tomorrow, I will enjoy my office and have a blessed day.

Lord, thank You for this day. Thank You for tomorrow.

6/28/2000 ~ 11:49 p.m.

Helping others is a blessing.

Yesterday, I had to speak with the students. One was physically and verbally abused by her husband. The other was verbally rude, using profanity to her classmates. Mr. Carr, CNA instructor, called me. I could hear the sorrow in his voice. His student had missed a week of class; she was an A/B student with good attendance. He had suspected physical abuse. When he saw her on Monday when she returned to school, she was sore. As I listened to this young 23-year-old lady, I studied her face and chestnut brown, swollen dark lips. Her face and lips quivered as she spoke. She could not express the pain in her heart as she tried to explain his action. Her husband had gone into a rage. He hit her in the face. After 8 days, the marks and bruises were still visible. I asked a few questions. He grew up in an abusive family. His father was physically abusive to his mother. She, the mother in-law, served 6 years for stabbing her husband. The student's husband referred to her as a bitch in the presence of his friends and their children. He was unemployed and didn't want her to continue in the CNA Program. After I counseled her, shared my personal experience of abuse and directed her to her mother. She was too ashamed to tell her mother. She had moved six months ago and she did not want her mother to think she was a failure. She was determined to make it. She had goals. We called her mother. She spoke to her mother. She knew something was wrong. She told her child to come home and they would talk.

The second student was a 38-year-old female. Her body language, her loud voice, the gyration of the neck, her need to break it down for me – all explained why she was referred to me. I stopped her coldly but passionately. I asked her age. When she said she was 38 years old, I explained to her simply this, "You are too old to break it down to me and I don't need such to happen." At 38, she needed to stop acting and speaking like she was 22 years old. She was a grown woman. Her language and movements prevented anyone from hearing her when the truth was being said, because she turned others off with her verbal abuse. As she listened, she stopped the language, the body movement; she sought words to speak more adult like. We spent 30 minutes together. She talked and told all – class activities, teacher's actions, etc.

She returned to class the following day. Mr. Carr called to say, "Thank you for whatever you said. She is a jewel, pleasant, so nice, a total 360 degree turn about." He presented her with a rose. She happily received it.

The Lord blessed me.

Wendy's father had a stroke yesterday. I called her and prayed with her. I hope my words comforted her. I called Charlie for support. He visited her. Today was Juanita's last day. It was unannounced and sudden to me. I was sad, but I understood. Her health required her attention. God had blessed the school with her presence. She had straightened up the Accounting Department. I will miss her. I cried softly, quietly in my office. Then I returned to work, keeping her departure to myself.

Goodnight, Lord.

7/3/00 ~ 10:37 p.m.

Time moves on. I am still unpacking. I made a commitment to review each folder. Items old not recorded would be discarded. I have thrown out boxes of papers, some dating back to 1993 and 1994. My files will definitely be thinner and current with pertinent items. I am preparing to revamp the organization. We need to grow. I will hire another instructor for MB/HCE, place Michael in recruitment, and create a marketing team: Alicia, Ann L., Margie, Mike and myself.

Linda L. Smith

Plans are underway for a Career Fair. Tutorial Program offered through friends, advertisement in theaters. Our enrollment is at 106. I pray to enroll a minimum of 30 students for the next start. We will enroll 20 students for the VN Class for July 17th – raising the total to 114. God can/will do it. I must take a closer look at the financials. We do have bills to pay and rooms to fill.

Next week – July 12th – is our 25th wedding anniversary. We have not made any plans. So Alicia is trying to get us to go to Tahiti. Short notice, high cost. We may end up some place else – Hawaii or Cancun. Actually, neither Ernell nor I seem too excited about going anywhere. My focus is so much into the school, his secretary is returning from medical leave. We may postpone the trip.

Aisha made the Dean's Academic List this quarter with a GPA of 3.5. We are very proud of her. It is worth supporting her. Lord, thanks.

7/8/00 ~ 8:11 a.m.

Yesterday the Capping and Pinning Ceremony was held at Four-D Success Academy. This was the 1st one held on campus. The activity room was huge enough to hold students and guests. I look forward to many, many more.

I received word from Al Twine that the new Administrator of Arrowhead Regional Hospital had pulled the contract. I placed a call to the Admissions office to speak to Mr. Uffer and requested an appointment for Monday or Tuesday. I know the outcome will be favorable for the school.

The ETP Monitor has interpreted the contract to read, "Only enroll 80 clients." We have a hold on our ability to pull more funds. I translate the contract to read, "Train 80." I know this will work in our favor.

200

The interest rate on our loan of $1,650,000 went up ½ percent. Must reflect a $593 increase. I know God did not get us here to financially fail. He will provide.

Thursday evening, I met with two sisters. Angela and Jeanette are a Placement/Marketing Director team. Respectfully, they have something to bring to Four-D Success. God bless this union if it is right for Four-D. Shield us from false presentation. Move us forward in spirit and in truth and love. Bless all You send to us. Bring them on one accord. Remove/shield us from sin and evildoers. I pray for the sick, lost, those in pain. Guide us to You.

Keep me. Keep Four-D Success Academy. Keep me humble, strong, and faithful.

7/12/00 ~ 10:10 a.m.

HAPPY 25TH ANNIVERSARY

We made it. Thank You, Lord. Today, Ernell and I rose to celebrate twenty-five years of marriage. Only God knows the challenges we've faced. Only God knows the past secrets of each of our hearts. Only God knows how to instill the full pardon of forgiveness. His love. He answered our prayers. Ernell and I are here today as husband and wife. We are off to Monterey for four days. We are going to have a wonderful time. I am very thankful to God, personally, for this blessing. My marriage is important. My husband, I need. Ernell is very good to me. This morning, we briefly talked about making the landmark. I expressed my desire to reach our 30th year. I have always wanted to be married 30 years. We discussed briefly celebrating our anniversary next year with a big trip. But I did get my RING at Christmas, my 2-carat marquee. I love it. As we ride in silence with the radio on low, I know our life is right for us. We are a team, we are partners, we are friends, we are lovers, and we are husband and wife. God is blessing us with 60 more.

Yesterday, the signs went up on the windows and doors. I was so proud of the school. It was our mark of ownership. The lamp. The name in full. All so very wonderful. The lobbies look elegant. Margie, Wendy, and Ann Logan have done a wonderful job in decorating them. The enrollment is picking up for the Medical Billing and Pharmacy Tech Class. I have prayed for 20-30 students in each program. He will provide. Thank You, Lord, for all.

7/16/00 ~ 10:05 a.m.

Well, the past four days with my husband have been wonderful. There's been lots of hand-holding, conversation, sex, love-making, walking, eating, and sightseeing. This was wonderful and RELAXING. I thought little of the school compared to previous trips. No writing or reading associated with the school. I even decided not to do the employees evaluation. My time and attention was on Ernell and me.

We stayed at the Sea Breeze Motel in Pacific Grove. It was a mile from the shoreline. We talked, walking the shoreline, taking in the beauty of God's ocean. We sat on the beach, facing the sea, looking at the glow crest the horizon as the sun set. Life for us is good, blessed by God. We celebrated our 25th wedding anniversary the right way, with hearts full of love for one another.

Lord, thank You.

7/21/2000 ~ 7:30 a.m.

Good morning, Lord.

Just a little note to say Thank You. I truly appreciate the time and attention You have dedicated to me. You have been patient, forgiving, compassionate, caring, loving, and supportive. I have made great personal and spiritual growth under your direction. You have been my greatest mentor.

As I travel the path You have prepared for me, I pray that I am as attentive to each step as you have been in its preparation. I pray that I continue to develop the spirit of discernment, the spirit of patience, and the spirit of joyful peace. I will strive to become a better wife, mother, boss, and person. I will strive to keep my smile genuine and my joy full. Each day, I will seek You for direction and support.

My home is happy with laughter and love. My husband and I look forward to the next 25 years of a loving, supportive marriage. My daughters have developed into fine, respectable, loving ladies. My business is successful in every sense of the word. We have achieved the goal (initial) you have set. We continue to pray, grow, and serve others. I thank You for the message of expansion that has come my way through others. Expansion of Friends – the non-profit organization, the expansion of the Academy as Thomas Windbush says, "I see you expanding to the next building. This whole area will be Four-D Success Academy."

I responded, "Thanks, let's agree in prayer for that in two years time. "Lord, that would be a great deal of growth for us. All things are possible through Christ Jesus, God our savior. All things. As I prepare to leave for work this day I pray for guidance. I pray that I am focused. I do not waste time or procrastinate. I pray for positive resolution on the ETP, ABHES projects. Lord, thank You for giving me this day. Each day is God's gift to us. How we live the day is our gift to God. Thank You, Lord. Your Child, Linda

7/23/00 ~ 11:22 a.m.

Away camping. Ernell and I went camping with friends Pete, Ballard's at Lake Silverwood along with Walter and Jeannie. We all had a relaxed and fun time. I missed the outdoors, blue skies at night, staring at the stars, coffee and bacon on the outdoors, and sleeping in the tent. I read, talked, laughed, and met new friends. It was all in fun. I even played cards. I had not done that in some time...

Back home, I prepared for tomorrow. I have a week to get the ABHES report out. I do hope the staff has completed the data I requested. I expect it to be complete. Then my work begins.

The payment on the mortgage went up $12,000 due to a ½ percent increase in interest. I immediately went to God. I know He did not place me and Four-D Success Academy in this building, knowing its increased cost, without a plan to help me. He will provide. He always has. There are many thoughts in my head; my weight, the school, my mother, my brothers, my children, life in general. God, I know, will help me resolve all issues. I must stay focused on the objective. Live right, do right, and be right – right with God. My feet have been swollen quite a bit this past week or two. At times, it is uncomfortable for me to walk just from the tightness when bending. I sometimes wonder if I create them in my mind. I remember when I was 16-17 years old while taking my CNA Training. I came across a patient at Del Rosa Hospital. She was short, arthritic, with fat swollen feet. I looked at her feet and wondered if my feet would ever look like hers. I hoped not. Whatever is the cause, I must remove it with prayer in mind.

Life is good. God is good, no matter what.

Lord, thank You for my life. I will strive to improve in all areas. Bless my tomorrow. I expect greatness and goodness.

7/25/2000 ~ 11:34 p.m.

Each day is God's gift to me. What I do with each day is my gift to God.

My gift today from God was another day to share. My gift to God was using Thursday to share with students in VN 12 the love of God, truth, and accountability He has given to each of us. After I shared the two sentences with the students, discussion followed on its meaning and how some students were not utilizing each day fully. Two students asked me to pray with them.

This is one of my greatest pleasures. I can openly pray for healing, faith, patience, elimination of fear, endurance, and all I desire. I can embrace sorrow, joy, tears, and laughter of students and faculty. God has blessed me with a wonderful environment.

I will rise early and apply time to writing the ABHES report. I will make the deadline. We all will overcome and achieve.

Thank You, Lord.

7/27/00 ~ 1:45 a.m.

Well yes, it is a new day and I am still up. I put into practice what I stress to the students. If you have to stay up to get the job done, then do so. I am working on the ABHES report. I am determined to have the report on Wendy's desk by the end of Thursday. I am 90% done.

Before I began writing, I sat and prayed. I was here working at home until 11:30 a.m. I had a marketing meeting at 12:30 until 2:30 p.m. Multiple calls placed. I continued to collect data from the ABHES report. Ann Logan and Alicia are gathering info on the employer's surveys. We must achieve 70% placement for the VN Program. We have achieved 71-73% placement on the PT Programs.

I received legal notice that the workers compensation claim is pursuing Jolene. I truly don't believe she is injured.

Financial Aid Title IV. Ann Logan said it will be fine. It was good to hear the positive comments come from her. It was a message of encouragement and God's omnipresence. Another valley, another test of faith.

I will be writing a letter to Eugene Gonzales to have the loan converted to a fixed rate. The variable rate has already increased our payment by $2,000.

Betty had to go to the hospital to be checked for hypertension. After she returned, she and I spoke. I inquired if the high blood pressure was due to work, but when she mentioned her kid in jail, that was all I needed to hear. Betty is repeating her vows on August 19th. She desires to have all of her children present. The news of jail rocked her, along with other personal issues.

God, protect all of us.

I will rise at 6:00 a.m. to attend court at 8:30. I am seeking payment on Health Department Service for Miguel's physical training.

Tomorrow/Today is blessed.

7/31/2000 ~ 1:50 p.m.

This is a glorious and blessed day – another gift from God. I think of His goodness, and I cry.

Today, while receiving prayer at Church, I was touched. As I held my hands in prayer, praying for family, brothers, friends, the GWC Organization, my husband, our marriage, our girls, Betty Thomas' wedding, I prayed for the school, for the students, for all staff. I prayed for wisdom to carry out the vision. I asked for direction, for prosperity. I prayed for the vision. A minister in the group touched my forehead with oil and prayed the same prayer. He verified in spirit what the Lord was saying and doing. I felt a rush go through me. I felt anointed, spirited. I was touched. As I journey through life, I wonder what God will do with me. My testimony is that He has used me according to His word. I believe in Him. He guides my path. My faith is my cement. It holds me firmly planted in God's presence in my life. My joy – I have no words eloquently to express. Just Jesus!

8/1/2000

We received a call on 7/31/2000 at 10:00 p.m. from Tahira. She/her home had been invaded. The thief entered through her garage door by lifting it up high enough to slip under. Since her door leading into her house was unlocked, it was easier access. Strangely enough, the police officer indicated the thief robbed on a Sunday – a low crime day. They did not vandalize the house, no damage, they did not remove the small appliances, TV, stereo. Later, Tahira noted 2 rings and $31 in change were taken.

Ernell fixed the handle which pulls the garage door down, removed the outside handle, and informed Tahira to lock ALL doors. We checked ALL windows. She informed the association and neighbors of the break-in. Ernell called an alarm company today for prices. The security front door will be up ASAP. I thanked God for my child's safety.

I can't wait to get the house in order at the school. The air conditioning is freezing in the Child Care. There is still a lot to do. Cash flow is tight. I had to go into the line of credit. Lord, help us. The student flow is not nearly where we need it. But we still exist. CPA Shawn Washington is in today for Audit Report. I must write. No time to be tired. No way. Lord, thank You for another day.

8/2/2000 ~ 12:47 p.m.

The alarm went off! My spirit had forewarned me last week. I was concerned that the alarm system was not working properly. I was worried of a break-in. I stressed to Wendy the need to have an operating system. Today, the police answered the alarm call. They used a knife to enter the south door up the stairs – used a knife to enter the 2nd floor. After searching the building, they exited the south door. As I arrived, they showed me the easy access. What to do to secure the building. I thank God nothing was taken. I contacted the locksmith. I had lock guards put into place, and went home.

Thank You, God.

8/3/2000

This is great. I have a pen with a light at the tip. I am writing in the dark. It was a gift from Ann Logan. When she showed me how it worked, I laughed and shouted with joy. I have been trying to write by the TV light. When Ernell is asleep, the lights are out, TV on, and

I'm writing. I use the low glow of the TV – but now I can see each word clearly. I see the lines and the tip of the pen. Ann, thank you.

The Lord has blessed us another day, another gift. I am thankful. Well, the night pen is not writing well. The light is great, but the pen is poor. I had an emergency meeting with the staff regarding security. I made myself clear.

I left work at 4:30 for a 5:00 hair appointment at the beauty shop. I planned for a short trip. I was out at 8:35 p.m. 3½ hours, but that's the price of time to look and feel better. I need a massage soon. Lord, I am sleepy.

Thank You. Goodnight.

8/6/00 ~ 11:29 p.m.

Tomorrow, I will be 48 years old. And though I have felt pretty good about myself, my size, looks, I have had a slight case of blues (depression). I told Ernell I wasn't pretty anymore. Saturday, I felt fat and old. I thought, *I am middle-aged. I have gray hair. I didn't lose a pound.* At one moment, I thought it was useless – eat the ice cream and cookies. I realized a sense of hopelessness, which lasted only a moment. An old acquaintance, Parker, and I talked briefly at Cayce's play. She complemented my hair, said it was gorgeous, lovely, white. I told her I felt old. All the ladies who like it wouldn't dare go gray. They all have black, brunette color, even Parker. Tomorrow, I will be 48. Gray or not, I thank God for my health and my life, the opportunities He has given me. Tomorrow, I will be 48. I have life and I have lived. I have experiences. I have memories. God, bless me to live another 48 years. After all, I have requested another 60 with Ernell. See you tomorrow. Happy Birthday, Linda. Love Ya!

7/8/00 ~ 11:00 p.m.

Yesterday was my 48th Birthday. Boy, what an emotional rollercoaster. I blew up with a support staff member. She had not completed an assignment, her work attire was unacceptable, and her attitude was poor. Another support staff was reprimanded about her attendance and punctuality.

Then I was surprised with gifts of a calming waterfall, incense, and a book on nutrition for working women. Tahira, my daughter, surprised me with roses and lunch. It was a delight to spend time with her.

Then I went to see Charlie Seymour. He and I stopped by Momma's house. He was going to place a lock on her storage. When I entered into her home, my stomach turned. Ronnie was back. His clothes and personal items covered the 1st bedroom. He began his usual rant of his accomplishments, a doctor, and his jaguar. While my mother and Charlie were outside, I calmly approached Ronnie in the living room. I started with, "This is not a shouting match. I want to ask you not to run Momma's telephone bill up. She does get upset when she is left with a high bill." His responses were loud. He was in denial. I should not talk to him like he's a criminal. He was like the brothers locked up, etc. Then he mentioned Fatu being like me, etc. I lit into him. I went into a rage. I cursed him, hit him, wished he would leave and not come back!

After departing, Charlie spoke with me. I listened, vowing to not 'go there' again with my reactions. Today, I called Momma to apologize for my behavior. It was the first time I had conducted myself so unbecoming in her presence. She said she understood my response to Ronnie. She herself wants to move away to get away from the tension. She is thinking of moving to Texas. At age 77, she still does not have peace and feels she needs to uproot and move with her 10-year-old grandsons 3,000 miles away.

I sat today in my office. The tears flowed briefly. I made arrangements with Wendy for Momma to fly to Texas for a visit at the end of the month.

The Allstate Ins. Company wants to decrease the lease space by 4/01. I am awaiting a response from Bank of California, County of San Bernardino, and Lee and Associates. The CPA is auditing 1997/1998 and 1999/2000 books. The tension is high for me. Take a deep breath and keep going. Lord, guide me.

Always call on Him.

8/11/2000 ~ 11:53 p.m.

Before I fall asleep, I will reflect on this day. I had not attended a social networking function for many months. I had been totally focused on the school. I dared not shift my thoughts to social gatherings. I had to maintain all my energy and keep a pinpoint focus on the survival of the school. But today, I decided to attend Congressman Joe Baca's 8th Annual Legislative Conference for Women. I am glad I did. There were old faces and new ones. I was greeted by old business friends and greeted by Congressman Baca, Senator Nell Soto, their staff, school district reps, and other business ladies. I became acquainted with others. I had my picture taken with the Congressman, Dr. Duneen DeBruhl, and a freelance photographer with the Sun Telegram took pictures of me (alone). I informed her of our Open House and requested coverage.

Back at the office, I made an emergency administrative decision – the Pharmacy Tech Program hours were changed and the length shortened – 8:00 a.m. to 2:30 p.m. – includes ½ hour lunch for 7-8 months. It is effective today. Alicia will adjust her program as necessary.

Margie Harris and I discussed the loss of clients not returning for financial aid review. She will talk with Ann Logan. I will receive a report upon my return. There are 22 candidates ready for the VN Program. Jean Stevenson must decide on the process for interviews and testing while I am gone.

Our funds are TIGHT. The line of credit of $150,000 is down to $9,000 in one book and $30,000 used from the line of $125,000. We have $100,000 – $120,000 left. We must generate enrollment immediately, repay the line by 3/2001, and pay large bills in the last quarter of the year. I have not received a response from Business Bank of California to convert the loan to a fixed rate. The County of SB has not signed the renewal. It should be done by the 16th.

I was reading the Business Press. There is an article on Computer Tech Training – the growing field. We have 30 new computers. I will talk with Thomas and Kadlil, offer quality training program for enrollment. We must grow and stay competitive. God, grant us wisdom. Guide me to the people who can help us. Keep our finances flowing. I want to provide a retirement plan to the staff by December of this year.

God, grant this blessing.

8/13/00

Today, Ernell, Aisha, and I attended the 10:00 a.m. service at Loveland. It was a blessing. A choir from Alabama sang. They lifted

212

our (my) spirits. I am so very thankful to God for His many rewards He has given me. I lifted my hands, extended my arms unto the Lord. Tears of joy, prayers whispered unto the Lord. We must hold on to God's unchanging hand. He knows the financial states of the school. He knows the bills we have and those to come. He knows the day of payroll. He knows where the students are, our efforts to reach out and help others. He knows our cares. We must hold on to God's unchanging hands. I pray for students. Triple the current number. I pray for a BIG, BIG financial blessing for all, the school, staff, and faculty. Lord, I do want to give out a raise in October. Please bless us greatly financially.

I ask the Lord for forgiveness. I lost control of myself. I said things I should not have to Ronnie. I can't change him but the Lord can. I pray for Momma's peace. I did apologize to her. She will be taking a short trip at the end of this month to Texas. I pray for her rest, health, and stamina.

The Lord is good – no matter what. Thank You, Jesus. Protect my child as You protect me.

Thank You. Your Child, Linda

8/19/00 ~ 4:28 p.m.

We left for Lake Mohave on Monday – Ernell, Jeanie, Walter III, Andre and I. We're going to the river with friends, a five-day fun-packed week of water, sun, boats, and food. New friends. As we headed out on Monday, I prayed for a safe journey for us all. I prayed for the school, for staff, and for students. Away for a week, all was in God's hands. The staff assured me things would be okay. The free day provided peace, a mind to think, a plan to grow, prayer and song time. I totally relaxed. By Wednesday, no phone, no pager.

I was relaxed. I am so grateful to God for my life. I have enjoyed this trip. It's been about five or six years since I was out on the boat or a group lake trip with Ernell. I am grateful for our life together.

I met Brenda and Jim. They live in Las Vegas. I told Brenda I am interested in opening a school in Nevada. She and I exchanged numbers. We will keep in contact.

We now travel home. Tomorrow is Betty and Calvin's big day. I am looking forward to the wedding and reception.

Lord, thank You for a blessed and safe trip.

8/20/2000 ~ 10:16 p.m.

You never know who is watching or listening to you. While exiting the Church ground, I was greeted by Gail – a young lady I have met in the choir. She informed me that she was inspired by my testimony. She had been trying to enter into the LA Police Academy. Many obstacles had blocked her path. But my testimony inspired her to stand fast. In September, she will enter the Academy. She said upon her completion of the Academy, she will give her testimony. I encouraged her to share her testimony before she graduates. Like my testimony helped her, hers will aid another. God blesses us to bless another.

The bills are mounting with the school. The funds are slowly coming in. I know God is ahead of us. He brought us this far and He will take us farther. As I reflect back over this past 12 months, I marvel at God's will.

We had a financial calamity – I thought, cancelled classes, due to low enrollment, cancelled VN classes, staff cuts – not replaced. The lowest enrollment. But we are still here. God is good – no matter what! Betty and Calvin Thomas renewed their vows at the 25th celebration. Her family, church members, and co-workers attended. She looked beautiful in her beaded sequin top white dress. Calvin was in a black tux. Ernell, Aisha, and I attended.

Tomorrow, I return to work after a week away. The school is still there.

Wednesday at 1:00 p.m., I will be in Palm Desert for the God's Women's Conference. I am looking forward to the blessing. Today, Charlene requested financial support for 25 young women. I asked for the financial blessing to support the young ladies. Aisha and I had a discussion last week. I told her I didn't have the $10,000 this year. She suggested I give $2,000 that will cover 25 young women at $75 each. At the time of her suggestion, we were not aware of the need to support 25 young women.

God already knows the outcome.

Time to prepare for tomorrow.

Lord, my God, thank You for the blessed week and this blessed day.

Tomorrow, the school will ultimately be blessed with multiple joys, gifts, students, and a positive outcome. Tomorrow will be a wonderful blessed day. I look forward to it. Thank You, Lord. Linda

Oh yes – the Nurse Consultant approved the school to enroll 45 students in October. We have come full circle. Jean Stevenson is doing a good job. The school VN Pass rate was 60%. That's a long way from 17% in January of this year, a significant improvement and damage control from her predecessors. Thanks, Lord!

8/23/00 ~ 12:20 a.m.

Glory to our God. He sits on high. Today, I am at the God's Women's Conference in Palm Desert. I am blessed. I work the tape ministry assisting to spread the Word of God. Oh, how blessed I am. I delight in His presence. I am healed, whole, and loved by God.

Today, before leaving the school, I brought the managers, faculty, and support staff together. I expressed Margie's concerns, the need to pray as a team and lift each other up. To lift the students up, to lift the school. I expressed the school was founded on prayer. It is sustained with praise. It will grow with prayer. We joined hands, led by Betty Thomas, a strong, spiritual prayer warrior for Christ. Kathleen followed, lifting us all up. Finally, I prayed. The tears flowed as I asked the Lord to heal the brokenhearted, remove all misunderstanding, and lift up the school. I gave thanks for Jean, her work, and all staff. I prayed for us all. I thank the Lord for all. God is preparing us for a huge move. Growth overflowing. Blessings come down. I thank the Lord.

The seed for the financial billing is planted, and the seed for the RP program is planted. The seed for the Child Care Center is planted. Now the seeds will grow and multiply. Lord, I thank You for Your guidance. I thank You for bringing those up to me to carry out Your work.

Lord, thank You for all. Bless each and every worker and person here at the Conference. Heal hearts, answer prayers in Jesus name, amen.

God's Women Conference

This year's conference is a blessing. We have been able to serve over 4,500 women and over 700 young adult women. The Lord is moving in a powerful way. Two to three weeks ago, the Lord put Charlene Singleton, Pres. of GWC, on my heart. I was thanking God for the school, for the funds to operate. As I thought of the Conference, I thanked God for the opportunity to reach the masses from behind the scene. My spirit was joyful as I saw the power of God through this ministry. I am able to give and sacrifice in the Lord to serve others. I am so thankful that my heart is pure in giving, my joy is helping others, and my blessing is aiding others in the ministry of the Lord. I realize that God is taking my unselfish heart, my desire to give assistance to others. He is directing my path. He has placed Charlene on my heart for a purpose. I am a servant to GWC. I didn't know how and what way until last night throughout the conference. I have been serving quietly in spirit. But I feel the Lord has not finished speaking with me. On Thursday, Carolyn Showell asked that we let the Spirit tell us what to give and to bring $300, if we could, in Spirit to the altar. I pulled out my checkbook and wrote the check for $300. That morning, I awakened, feeling the spirit of God. He had told me to give Mother Alice Williams $200. He told me I had it. My mother had left the money for me at her home. I had paid for her ticket to fly to Texas for $425. She insisted on paying it back. I said, "Momma, give me $200 dollars and you keep the rest." The Lord told me to give Mother Alice the $200. On Wednesday morning, I wrote the check and placed it in my bag. I went to work. At the end of the day, Mother Alice came to the tape ministry to turn in a lost Bible for me to take to the information desk. I quietly handed her the check and continued to work. No words spoken other than, "I am being obedient to the Spirit of God." Thursday morning, Beatrice Gardiner ministered to us at the end. She asked that we be still and let the spirit minister to us and to tell us what to give. My Spirit said, "Write the check for $1,000." I did. Then she, (Beatrice) said to write Love Offering on it. I did, and submitted it.

Last night, Juanita Bynum spoke a powerful message. Her interpretation was like no other. Jesus at the well with the Samaritan Woman. At the end of the message, she told Charlyn that the Lord was going to expand her ministry to work with another more distressed group. At that moment, the Lord filled me. "That is what you are to do. Support this ministry. Serve the multitude through Charlyn. I will bless you financially because you are not foolish with my blessing that I have given to you. You have stayed the course. I have raised you up so that you may serve others through me."

As I walked and looked around, I thought of the two-bedroom house and the nine people at 1450 Mt. Vernon. I thought of my life, the path I have been on, the people I have been touched by. I looked at 4,000 women and the Lord told me, "I have given you riches to serve ME. The millions of dollars belong to me. You have been faithful. You have served me well. You will be blessed." I prayed and thanked God. I could see where I am to go. The path is already established by God. Charlyn will serve the multitude and I am to supply the financial support to aid her mission in doing the Lord's work. We all have an assignment. We all can't be in the front. Someone has to walk in line behind the leader and do it with joy. I count this all joy.

The Lord is blessing us. He is going to move FDSA in a powerful way. The building will be paid off in the name of Jesus in five years, all $1,600,000 in the name of Jesus. He will guide our path. The Lord has set us in our own building. We are the youngest school, with the smallest enrollment, but we bought the largest building. The Lord is moving in a powerful way.

Lord, I thank You for Your love, for the vision. Thank You.

Live in obedience to Your Word Lord. Your Child, Linda

8/27/00 ~ 12:03 a.m.

A Firm Foundation – that's the title of Dr. Charles Stanley's month book for September. How appropriate for how I feel. The conference, the presence of the Lord, my covenant with Him, the school, the future. God's support of us. A firm foundation.

I listened to Darlene Bishop and Charlyn Singleton's tape on the drive home from Palm Desert. Once I got on the freeway – 10 west – I set the speed control to 69, took my feet off of the control pedals, and relaxed. From Palm Desert to the Montclair Indian Hill exit, I cruised ALL the way – listening to the powerful messages from the women of God.

Once home, I placed a call to Tahira. I had a tape to deliver. Aisha had spoken to me regarding my responsibility to discuss Tahira's life with her. Even though Tahira is on her own, I am her moral guide. Aisha felt I needed to discuss personal life. Juanita Bynum provides clarity to assist me. I shared the conference with Ernell and Aisha. Oh what a joyful time I had. I know I am in the will of God.

Thank You, Lord. Love You.

Linda L. Smith

8/29/00 ~ 11:00 p.m.

Lead me, guide me.

God's protection abound. As I continue to assess the financial situation. I see our income dropping. Yet, God is good.

He sees our need. I sing, pray for more students, for wisdom, and for focus. I am obedient to spiritual messages. I wrote a letter to Charlyn Singleton expressing God's will in my life to support GWC/Ministry financially. I informed the Accounting Department of the added financial obligation. I know, without any doubt, God is willing this to be. I know He will reward us. Today, Frank Doughty from the Riverside *Press Enterprise* provided direction for Marketing. We owe $8,000 for pass advertisement. Our paper was being prepared to go to an attorney for collections. But the papers were placed on Frank's desk and I advised he take care of it. God intervened for us. Frank convinced the group the debt need not go to the attorney. We had been making monthly payments in good faith. He will speak on our behalf and request that our ad run with the intent of gaining students to pay off the debt by December 2000.

Each day will be a blessed day. I reminisce about the summer of 1992. Charles Williams from the Council for Private Post Secondary approved the school. A blessed day!

I know we have much to do. I can feel the positive energy. The open house, a new class in October of 45 VN students. Reassignment of faculty. Mike Williams is working with Margie in Admissions. A new employee providing remediation to ATB clients, Cathy in the VN Program. God has His mighty hand on us.

Ernell and I are seeking new tenants. The county signed a month-to-month note. We pray for a 5-year lease with another medical group. The Child Care Center will be underway in January 2001. God is good.

8/30/2000 ~ 11:38 p.m.

I'm seeking new tenants. I called Charlie and gave an update on the school's status. I informed him I was seeking tenants for the All State and Clinic Suite. Within 30 minutes, he was in my office with Leroy Baker, his son-in-law. Leroy had stopped by Charlie's place to pay a debt. During their conversation, Leroy mentioned his company was seeking a location in the Riverside area or Colton. We have the Allstate Suite. The size is perfect, location great. Charlie will take pictures for Leroy's presentation.

I called Irene Sandoval and Dr. Hess for referrals for the Clinic. I had to speak with 6 students in class, 12 who had less than 75% in their class course work. All were subject to fail the program if they did not earn 75% on the Muscle Skeletal System. I first informed them of my concern – the possibility of failing. Then, I discussed/lectured on how to avoid it. Motivation is a big part of what I do, not threatening. I shared God's love and their intellectual possibilities, interferences, goals, being visionary, seeing themselves as qualified, safe practicing, licensed Vocational Nurses. Following the 'talk,' I told the ladies, "You know I believe in the power of prayer." We joined hands and I prayed for each lady.

God is good.

Mr. Sam Teo informed me he had made an appointment for me to see the MD in Chief of Rehab Medicine from Arrowhead Medical Center. Confused, I thought the doctor was first coming to represent the hospital. Then, I realized Mr. Teo had made arrangements for me to meet a friend of his. Clarity was to come. I met Dr. Robert Kanuage,

221

MD Chief of Rehab Medicine. Robert is Indonesian. His interest was to bring Indonesians here for education. Arrowhead had rejected the idea. I am interested. We discussed the process and possible number of students to come, the I-20 process, etc. After our meeting, I was excited. I was excited about all of the possibilities of having an international arm for training. We scheduled to meet on September 11th. We also discussed Medical Billing Services.

All of these wonderful possibilities are REAL. God will make this happen.

Today, I signed Payroll Checks. The rent, other bills – all paid. I am so very thankful to God for His continued blessing.

I prayed with students, discussed a possible international venture, and attended Choir rehearsal.

I am blessed. Goodnight, Lord.

9/1/00 ~ 12:00 Midnight

Pushed over the edge. The CPA report final was $49,000 plus interest owed to the Department of Education for misappropriate/overdrawn funds under the past financial aid directions for the 1997-1998 year. The cost for the audit is $4,000 and he is going to bill us over two months. He has yet to complete the Annual Audit at $3,600 and corporate tax cost unknown. We have to mail $2,650 to the Bureau associated with the mandating fee of (STRF) $5,210 to the Bureau for the annual fees and $4,000+ to ABHES for annual fees. Up to $20,000 or more for fees to be in business. Tears swallowed, as I know the Lord is providing. We did not have to use any line of credit for the 1st of the month's bills. Thank the Lord. The plumber did not come. I have had cancellation 3x all week. Today, I received a call at 3:30 from his wife to inform me he is on his way after I had called him at 1:00 p.m. But he is in slow traffic heading east. He will arrive at about 4:30 and wants staff to stay over. I am livid. Then he is unable to come on Saturday between 8-12. therefore he will be in on Tuesday. I called Mary Ellen and raised a little hell. She received an ear-full. I told her I wanted a check, the balance owed to the plumber. I would get my own plumber to complete the work. I was extremely angry. God, forgive me, but I am tired of being put off and lied to.

My car is in the shop. The cost for repairs is about $2,500. The power steering is gone, the windshield wiper motor is gone, belts need replacing, front brake pad needs replacing, coolant needed, and something else. The car will remain in the shop until Wednesday a.m. But I got a Jaguar 2000 S with 18 miles as a loaner. Navy blue, small, and cute – but not my red, big, smooth Jaguar. Anger displaced, I sought peace in my spirit. Classical music 105.1 played softly as I drove from West Covina to Fontana. Relaxing, calming upon arrival at Church for Choir rehearsal. I found members fellowshipping. It is a reunion. Members (old) have returned to sing in a concert on Sunday evening at the Ontario Convention Center. It is good to see so many faces and to be in the midst of the Lord's praises. Pastor D Crawford told me, "Not many can do what you are doing. When they say you can't, you can and keep going. When they say don't, you do and keep going. I know you will. I know what it is like. I've been there. That's why I can admire you. You are making history. They write about people like you."

I gleamed at his words. Who will write about me in history? I don't know and I don't care. I am so pleased to do my work for the Lord. All praise goes to Him. Those who are not pleased – I am sorry but I have tried my best. I know God is pleased. He keeps us open. I am in awe of His words. We have 99 students and payroll was met. I dreamed God would take us down to 100 students. Then, we would see an explosion of students. I see 400 students on campus. I know it can be done. We are increasing our marketing through theaters. It will be seen 9/27 in the SB 20 Star Cinema. Also in *Job Guide*, *Press Enterprise*, *Employment Guide*, *Penny Saver*, TV, and word of mouth. It will happen. I will start a Computer Training Course with Thomas. The Child Care is coming and a Medical Billing Service. God will provide.

Lord, I want to give the entire staff a raise of 10-15%. Helps us find a solid financial foundation and spread our wings. Thank You for Your protection and love.

9/1/00 ~ 8:15 a.m.

The Message

The last dream of the night. The time? I don't know. The dream: I am walking through a bazaar. I am not quite sure of what it is but I see myself exiting a door. Outside the door is a table with pamphlets on health issues. I see a pamphlet on blood pressure. I start to take several for the upcoming Health Fair that will be held on September 17th at Rialto, put on by Loveland Church. But, I decide not to take the information. My thoughts are to go inside and talk with the ladies.

As I look up, a lady comes to the table and asks if I received a mug. I say, "No." She invites me back in. As she hands me the cup, she tells me the Lord has His hand on me. I don't say what I do, and she does not ask. As she hands the cup to me, she looks to the other ladies and they acknowledge that the Spirit of the Lord is upon me. I radiate with a smile. I say, "Thank you." I am told all is well. There is such acknowledgment from these ladies. There is repeated, "Yes – yes she is." I feel the warmth within me. The message – everything is going to be all right. 99 students, bills paid. What do these ladies see – messages from God? Don't worry, don't fret. He takes care of all things. Holding the cup, I embrace the Spirit. The words penetrate my soul. Peace within, calmness.

As I exit the room with a smile upon my face, I hear the voice of Aisha, "Coming for Mama. It's time to get up. Get ready for the Church picnic. We are part of the set-up team."

God is good – no matter what. We move forward in life always in the presence of the Lord.

I am so blessed for knowing this. Lord, thank You.

Your forever-thankful child,

9/4/00 ~ 11:04 p.m.

My first thoughts deal with a compliment a friend gave me last week. He said I was the most beautiful woman he had ever met. The look on my face expressed my thoughts. But he restated his comments. Now, I have known this man for more than 20 years. His previous wife and female companions are all light-skinned and weigh at least 50-80 lbs. less than me. He provided a clear statement of my character and personality.

I treat everyone the same, how I carry myself, my smile. I was quite stunned at such words. At my 'peak' weight, I was found most attractive. Now, I know my husband loves me big time. I am his wife. Life goes on. I take the compliments with grace, smile, and say, "Thank you."

Last night was Loveland Gospel Reunion Concert. It was great being back in the choir. About 160 singers performed at the Ontario

Convention Center. My husband and girls were in attendance. I was pleased.

I prayed for more patience and internal peace. I have been so angry with the contractors. I feel I am a female African-American – not extremely vocal about my feelings until I am very angry. Then I voice myself to another woman – Otis' assistant – Mary Helen. I have not heard from Business Bank of California about a request to provide a fixed ratio. But I know God will provide. There is so much to do. I need to become better at managing my time and projects. I have not made calls regarding additional business. RN Programs, partnership with colleges, Valley, Child Care Center, Medical Billing Services, Increase Enrollments.

God, guide the staff and me. Aisha has put me on a 'fast.' I have to eat 3 meals a day for 30 days. I do not eat well-balanced meals. I will stay with it. Tomorrow starts the fast. Today, I ate 2 meals and walked for 20 minutes, a few stretches. I am quite big, at least 200 lbs. Now, I KNOW what I look like. 4 years ago, I questioned what I would look like at 200 lbs. Now, I know I wear a size 14 in pants, and most tops. I have fat distributed all over. I really don't look too bad. In fact, there are days I think I look rather good. But I know I will feel better if I lose 50 lbs. I watched my weight go up – now I will work it down.

God, keep me focused in all things.

9/7/00 ~ 4:50 a.m.

Awakened to the sounds of water dripping. I think, in a daze, *It can't be raining.* Thoughts of my call from Irene Sandoval cross my mind. Irene called me yesterday afternoon with the recommendation to write a letter to a Kaiser Administrator to inform him of the availability of the clinical space. Awakened by the water sprinklers actively clicking as the Vale Park grounds are being watered, followed by my own backyard water sprinkles becoming active. I focus on a draft letter to the Hospital Administrator. There is so much for me to do. I can't afford to waste time. Lord, I thank You for waking me up. I pray You guide my thoughts to write. Provide clear, concise statements of understanding. Thank You. Good morning, Lord. Linda

9/7/00 ~ 11:00 p.m.

Same day blessing. I rose early to draft my letter to Kaiser Hospital Adm. Once I completed the draft, Ernell returned to bed. He had risen, without my knowing, and had planted himself on the couch in the den. I turned the TV to channel 40 TBN and began listening to Joyce Meyers, drifting off to sleep. Ernell returned to bed at 5:30 a.m. and we held each other, falling into a deeper sleep. I awakened again at 6:30 a.m. to the voice of John Hagee preaching on "It is sinful to be fearful. What is there to be afraid of if God is with you? Don't let sinister thoughts penetrate your mind." Oh so true. God is ALWAYS with us. There is nothing that can separate us from God. Staying in faith and trusting in the Lord has brought me this far. I KNOW God is providing all our needs.

Otis Lacey came by with D.J. to discuss the final touches. He knows I am skeptical. I informed him I had plans to paint myself on Saturday. He is supposed to be at the school at 7:00 a.m. with a crew. I will wait and see. I received the call from Eugene Gonzales, V.P. from Business Bank of California. The Board approved my request to change the variable loan to a fixed loan at 11%. The note at 10.5% was $12,984 interest only. When it rose to 11% (1/2 pt.) the note rose to $15,000. I now expect the rate to be at $17,000 fixed at 11% for principle and interest. Lord, thanks for this blessing.

Our student population continues to decline as students graduate. 16 students were moved from the roster by the registrar having an enrollment of 89 students. The enrollment for the VN program is progressing slowly. We have about 25 of the 45 allowed.

The enrollment into the Pharmacy Tech is 11 students in class and 4 in the field. I am praying for insight to correct this block. We must enroll students to keep that program alive. Last year, we generated $120,000. I know we will recover.

Well, Lord, it's time for me to sleep and rise early. I truly am expecting a wonderfully blessed day. Lord, guide me into the future. How do I plan for growth changes? Keep me focused, give me wisdom.

9/10/2000 ~ 10:56

This past Saturday and Sunday, Ernell, Avendel, and I prepared God's House, His gift to me and Ernell for the City of Colton's final review on the Open House. We worked on the environment, cleaning carpet, hanging doors, bulletin boards, touch up paint, furniture, hauling out old items. I so very much want a large turnout. I know it is blessed. On Saturday, we worked from 9:00 a.m. to 9:00 p.m. Back on Saturday at 10:30 until 4:45 p.m. Avendel was great. He came back and worked with Ernell to satisfy my spirits. I thanked both of them so very much. I am anxious. The staff has performed well with minimal guidance. Kim (Howard) will bless us with song. The caterers are lined up; the photographer, David Perry, is ready. The guest judge needs to show up. Lord, bless us this week, and each week of the year 2000. As we move forward, God's presence is upon us. He has brought us this far by faith. I know God has His hand on me. He has changed me. I have been transformed! My faith and my trust in God continues to bless me every day. Lord, there are ideas/projects I must do. You have laid ideals upon my heart. I pray for focus, the process, the foundation to say, "Through God, all things are possible." Thank You for allowing me to bless others. As I cleaned my furniture, I touched the marble engraved with the signatures for the very first class of CNA – 1991. We have come a long way. Lord, thank You.

Loving You Always.

9/12/00 ~ 11:00 p.m.

I can't wait to receive the approval from the City of Colton. The Fire Marshal and a city inspector walked through on Monday, unplanned and underestimated by the constructor. The sprinkler system had not been approved by the Fire Marshal – the final approval from the City. The persons in charge were kind and considerate. They will work with the contractor. The Open House will occur tomorrow.

The Open House is tomorrow. All is planned. I know the staff has done everything to prepare us for this two-hour moment. I know we are going to move forward. About 600-700 invitations were mailed. I have received 8 returns. Gifts are ready. The photographer, singer, and caterers are ready. It is blessed.

Tomorrow, Ernell and I are going to set up our booth for the African-American Village. Tomorrow is a full day.

Today, Dr. Kanuaga and I discussed Indonesia. The door is open for a bright future.

I talked with my nephew Kaleid who was in the hospital after passing out on Saturday. He is okay. We talked about God's path for His life. Lord, thank You.

9/13/00 ~ 11:39 p.m.

OPEN HOUSE DAY

I awakened early, thoughts racing through my consciousness. *How will the Open House turn out? Who will show up? Is the school ready?* I wondered what Margie's décor will look like. I lay next to Ernell, cuddling his chest. As I thought of the journey of my life, the tears streamed across the bridge of my nose. Weeping silently, I thanked God for all that has occurred. Now today, we were having our Open House. We were going to show off Four-D Success Academy – our home, God's gift to us. I said a prayer while the staff prepared for the Open House. Ernell and I prepared for the set up at the 1st Annual African-American Village to be held in the 78-year history of the Los Angeles Pomona Fair. The excitement is in the air. 52 vendors, performers, and a guest visit by Presidential candidate Al Gore and George Bush. Ernell was a General. He set up our booth, laid the carpet, hung the banner, and lights. Once we received our tickets from JoAnn, we left to prepare for the Open House.

When I arrived at 5:00 p.m., the hostess had already begun the tours. The guests were provided a script of the school layout. The school looked GOOD. Every room was in order! The caterer's food was good. The hostess and staff dressed in black. We were very impressive.

Recognition was received from Supervisor Jerry Eaves by Al Twine and Assemblyman John Longville by his representative. There were too many guests to name here. But we also had the presence of my mother and mother-in-law, family members, the Colton Police, the

City Department Development, All State Rep, City and County WTA Reps, and many more. I was blessed in song by Kim Paulie, Shirley's daughter. She sang a song of glory. The words touched my heart deeply. "All I need is the Lord." The message clear to me was God's reinforcement. All I need is Him – continue to trust in God. We will reach 400 students (minimum). I thank the Lord for this day. Tomorrow, we begin recruiting for the African-American Village. I am praying for 400 referrals and students.

Thank You, Lord. A Grateful, Blessed Child, Linda

9/15/00 ~ 8:00 a.m.

Long hours at the fair trying to recruit clients. Traffic was very light. We only signed up 3 people. On Thursday, we signed up 16. But last evening was a good time to listen to Mike Williams, the Director of the Medical Billing Program. He had a whole lot to say about everything pertaining to recruitment. He has good ideas. He is aggressive and needed. He also shared his concerns of the housekeeping service and how much they get paid. Now that spooked my ear. Only Wendy and Pat know that. When he said Wendy, I became angry. She is sharing personal and confidential information. How much else is she sharing of the finances and info from my office? I am surely going to address this with her in writing. Today, I am going to attend a Fashion Show with my mother and Betty. Then I am going to the fair from 4-10 p.m. Tomorrow, I will be at the fair from 10-10. It's the last day to recruit. I pray to quadruple the numbers - that means I want at least 1,100 clients minimum. I know we will be all right. God is moving us in the right direction. Thank You, Lord. Linda

Linda L. Smith

9/18/00 ~ 11:30 p.m.

Tahira is 24 years old.

Twenty-four years ago, I entered into labor with my first child. I remember my "plug coming," light water running down my leg. But I was not having any labor pain. After a while, I called my mother and explained what had occurred and listened to her excitedly tell me to get to the hospital. I decided to wait until the labor pain was 10 minutes apart. Came they did, and I felt as though I was going to pass a basketball. The pain was unspeakably tremendous. As Ernell and I headed to Kaiser in Fontana, the ride seemed endless. The pains were close. The rectal/pelvic pressure was a killer. I thought if I could stretch my body, I could handle the 'basketball.' Tahira came after about 5 hours of labor. I tried to go all the way without medication. But, once again, the pain was THE PAIN. Natural birth was not going to happen. I finally requested an epidural to tolerate the delivery with Ernell present in the labor room. I gave birth to a beautiful baby girl. We named her Tahira Ayanna Smith – the pure beautiful flower. Today, she is a pure beautiful flower, a mature, independent, loving, young lady. God has blessed us. He has given us a jewel. Lord, thank You.

Today, I shared the vision with the management staff. I had to express the vision and the financial status of the school, God's protection, the tension I have sensed, and how it hurts the school and productivity. I stressed the need to move forward. No overtime and why. 89 students at $1,000 and $89,000. Payroll is $90,000 a month. This does not cover Adm. cost/operations. I think I got their attention.

Then I presented the plan to expand in Las Vegas, Nevada by 2001. There is much to do. The seed is planted.

Tomorrow is a new day. I am ready. Goodnight, Lord.

Thank You.

9/19/00 ~ 11:50 p.m.

The day was blessed. Five students in Class 11 passed their finals. They graduate at the end of this month. I am so excited for them and for the Academy. The Department of Education's final findings were for the Academy to return about $49,000 back due to errors of previous Financial Aid Directors, Steven and Theresa. I received a call from Lorena, River Beaumont Gain office. She will accept referral for CNA/Training. Betty and I forge ahead tomorrow. I was informed that there is "a lot of money" to spend. As I continued to work into the evening, I opened my mail. There was a letter and 2 complete contracts from Kaiser Permanente Hospital for all 14 hospitals and clinics from L A to Riverside. Neither Jean nor I had met with Kaiser. A staff nurse had inquired, we think. All I have to do is sign the contract tomorrow and mail with proof insurance. This is God-sent. We received the South Bay Contract for the VN Program with the $19,575 rate. Their clients from another school have applied for transfer. Students with solid grades. This is a blessed day. And yes, I spoke with Delores Weld about a fast-track RN Program. We will make it. Thank You, Lord.

9/22/00 ~ 11:56 p.m.

Oh what a day. The events leading to success is awesome. This was a busy day. From 7:45 a.m. until 9:00 p.m., I worked. Appointment after appointment. Walk-ins, discussions by telephone and fax. The team is in motion. Mike is following up on the I-20 process. Amber has begun the search on programs and schools in Las Vegas via the Internet. Priscilla has contacted the Vegas Chamber of Commerce to obtain demographics. Jerry Green (I met at the African Village) called and referred me to Ken Evans in Las Vegas. Ken is involved in Community Development. We talked about my goals to establish a school in the Vegas area. He provided the names of 3 significant individuals. He felt they could assist with the process.

Wendy will send Bio info to him for review on Tuesday. I will meet with Kim on the October 21st weekend while in Vegas. I spoke with Darrell in Beaumont. He informed me that there was concern that we were not approved to teach our CNA/HHA program in Riverside. I immediately knew that Carrie Somebody was trying to stir up problems. I faxed our approval from DHS and gave him the phone number to Howard Maralami. The Lord is nurturing our seed to grow. We have about 22 students fully approved for the VN 10/16 class. 7-10 awaiting IRIS approval. We have received transfers from another school. We will have 20 more for this VN Program. The enrollment for the Medical Billing and Pharmacy Tech program will increase.

Today, I met with Barbra Brenson, Marketing for Rehab Clinics. She is positive she can help me. I will know within a month. Ms. Garland attended the Riverside Child Care Meeting. I will follow up on Tuesday with her.

Lord, there is much for me to do. I pray You keep us focused as a team. Bless each of us and answer our prayers. Thank You.

9/27/00 ~ 1:58 a.m.

Well, the Lord keeps on blessing us. Yesterday at 1:50 p.m., Ernell and I signed the revised Term Agreement with Business Bank of

California. The fixed interest rate is 11%. The monthly rate is $16,178.27. We were told that, to the knowledge of Jay Smith and Eugene Gonzales, the board in its history has never changed a signed agreement before a 2-year period, and the client must make perfect payments. We received a revised term agreement after a request two months into signing. God blessed us. I am expecting excellent results from the Marketing efforts of Barbara Brenson. Vocational Rehab Clients will fill us. Today, I spoke with Howard Maralami, State Consultant. We needed to submit a letter to move the approval training site from Community Hospital to Beaumont School along with Sui Rukert's papers. Darrell Brown was notified as well as Ken. We plan to start a new program in 2 weeks. Lord, continue to protect us. Goodnight. 2:16 a.m.

9/27/00 ~ 12:00

The ABHES Report was resubmitted for the 2nd time (this go round). Wendy, Pat, and I laid hands on it, said a prayer of acceptance and Fed-Ex'd it to Virginia. Tonight, I watched T.D. Jakes "Women Thou Art Loosed." The ministry blessed me. Loose is free, free in the spirit of God. Blessed. Called by name to do my pre-destined assignment. I am loosed. No worry, He is with me. No crying, no stopping me. No, no, no. For I am loosed. God has a plan for me. He already knows my name, where I am going, who will try to stop or interfere, and who will help. He already knows I will be successful in sharing the Word. Today, I shared with Ronald, a student, to graduate tomorrow. He thanked me, said God would bless me and embrace me. I am free to share my love of God, of Jesus. I am free – loosed. Lord, I thank You for payroll, for the staff, thank You. Bless us with students. In Jesus name, amen.

Linda loves the Lord and the Lord loves me.

9/30/2000 ~ 9:28 p.m.

Filled with anger, head throbbing, blood rushing, trying not to drown. Yesterday, a 'client' brought her book to the receptionist window to announce she was dropping from the MB/HCE class. She was turning in her books. I had her see Margie in Admissions. Low and behold, she was never enrolled into the school. She and another 3 ladies had attended class under Mike's instructions – unofficially. I was beyond livid. He, once again, had violated school policy.

Unable to contact him, I immediately wrote a disciplinary note on him. I will see him on Monday. Another violation and he will be terminated without question. Pat and I discussed the Medical insurance coverage. I listened, considered the recommended plan. She called Ernell and told him we had decided to change. Upon arriving home, he was COLD towards me. Then he hit me with the question, "If I was not satisfied with the coverage, why didn't I tell him?" I had absolutely no idea what he was talking about. He then said something about me cutting him out. I asked why didn't he call me and ask what I was doing, thinking? He didn't. Why not call? After 25 years, he still lacks the ability to talk openly and frankly with me. I was puzzled, hurt, and angry. He was watching the Olympics and could not talk with me. I went to bed. What a day.

Today, I met Ms. Tee for breakfast at 8:30 a.m. I returned home at 2:30 following my hair appointment. Aisha wanted us to talk. We both came into the room. His words and his attitude drove me to the edge. I made an honest mistake. I could not get him to understand. I am overwhelmed. I am the manager. I make all decisions. I made an honest mistake. I forgot he was the agent on the Medical Insurance.

Overwhelmed and hurt, I left to be alone. I went to the movies. From 3:00-8:00, I watched movies.

Upon leaving, I just sat in my car. I opened the well and let the well empty a little. There are times I am lonely. I asked the Lord to show me the direction to go. Bring the students to grow, to serve. What am I not doing right? The census is now 65 students, fifteen graduated on Friday. In two weeks, we will have a new class. I can only wait for the final enrollment. In my car I prayed, cried, and felt lonely. The road I travel is traveled by few. I will stay on my path. God is my success.

Thank You, Lord.

10/5/00 ~ 11:28 p.m.

Michael knew I was looking for him. He had multiple calls from his fellow employees. He approached me, said, "I want to talk to you now." I immediately informed him I was going to talk to him – in my office. Upon entering, I told him to have a seat. He said, "NO." After 2 or 3 times of telling or asking him to sit, I became angry and informed him he was not going to stand over me. "Sit, or leave my office." He sat. I handed him my write-up. His response led to fire from me. He yelled, criticized others, and cried. In disbelief, I sat, handed him a tissue to wipe his face and blow his nose. He could not see what he had done. The confusion he created, trying to enroll students. He cried, said he was going to tell his wife. He came here to help the school, but I find he doesn't want to follow policy. I made it clear that policy would be followed. He informed me he would not participate in recruiting students. One person does not stop the ship. Today, I met with Aja, Margie, Tamika, and Mariana. I explained new strategy for enrolling clients, a total team effort. We will move forward. Today, I met with Llana Hall, Education Coordinator for Molina Health Care in the corporate office in Long Beach. We discussed the Academy, and the goal to provide Education Training to the Med Assistant and Medical Billers. I will call her next Friday to find out how things progress.

Alicia is working on getting contracts for IV Training with Pharmaceutical Company.

Goodnight, Lord.

The DHS approved the Beaumont as a training site.

10/9/00 ~ 11:58 p.m.

We received the DHS approval for Beaumont School. I still need the approval from the Bureau of Private Post Secondary and Voc. Ed School. I know it will come and everything will work out. Mike, Margie, and I attended the Riverside Conference. I was able to see the energy of each. Mike talked almost the entire time, collected information, cards, expressed new ideas. Margie had little to say. I think she fed on his energy and could see his networking skills and ideas. I met Leonora and Salinas of the Riverside WIA Offices. Positive contracts. Leona will screen and enroll students into the CNA Program.

The ABHES group gave permission for me to mail the audit late. The report will go Wednesday evening. I have an appointment on 10/30 to discuss the RN Program with Delores Weld and meet with Ken Smith in Las Vegas on Friday 10/20. I know this will turn out positive. Well, its 12:21 a.m. I have an appointment with Barbara Brenson and a Vic Rehab Case Manager.

Goodnight.

Michael and I had a long talk (5-8). Good stuff. I am sleepy.

10/11/00 ~ 9:28 p.m.

Surprise – South Bay must approve the Beaumont site. I had to sit still and know that everything would be okay. Ken and I talked. I will rent a van to transport the students to Colton. Things will work out.

Time to work at the computer.

Thank You, Lord.

10/12/2000

Dorothy Ivery – she brought tears to my eyes.

While quickly walking out of the campus greeting students, I came upon an elderly lady sitting in the lobby. As I approached her, I smiled and said, "Hello." It was my momma's greeting. I asked if she had been helped. As she looked at me and smiled, we extended hands to shake. She clasped my right hand between the two of hers and asked, "Are you the lady in the picture?" I answered, "Yes, ma'am."

She responded with a thrill. The look in her eyes was different. The touch of her hands holding mine was different. She stated how happy she was to meet me. She said she had heard of me and was determined to meet me one day. She was proud of me. "One of us is doing something good like this." She then asked for a picture of me. Nothing big, she could have it blown up. She was going to hang it on her wall. I laughed as I said, "Sure, I'll get one." She asked that I mail it to her once I found a picture of any size. Her name was Dorothy Ivery. She printed her name so that I could read it clearly. I felt like a celebrity. She wanted my signature on the picture. As I walked towards my office, it was not the feeling of stardom, but pride. Pride in the effect I was having on the lives of others. I was doing good for Dorothy Ivery. She was proud of me for being a young black woman and doing something good.

As I kneeled and prayed to God, tears flowed. I was taken a step deeper into the realm of my role in this life. As I serve the Lord, my Jesus Christ, I touch the hearts of strangers. I am protected at Four-D Success Academy by the Lord.

We will continue to serve the Dorothy Ivery's of this world. God chose me. He called me by name and I answered.

I am so very blessed to serve. Lord, I thank You. Keep us. Protect us. Let us continue to rise above all obstacles. Ms. Dorothy Ivery, thank you for the message. Thank you for the tears of joy, love, determination, and pride in self.

Thank You.

10/19/00 ~ 11:14 p.m.

Calmness and peace is about me. Release everything to God. Do the best I can and know everything will be all right. The financial woes, Shawn, CPA. Estimate a financial loss of $50,000-$100,000 for the year. The Department of Ed requires I repay $140,000 from 1997/1998 and 1999/2000 audits. Yesterday, I spoke with Dianne Wittman, reviewer at Department of Ed. If I can find any errors in the audit, I must submit them before November 15th. I checked one chart and found an $8,000 error by the CPA. Ann and I will review every file for errors and request another review. Today, Jeff came by Voc. Rehab Riverside County. He was impressed with the school. He left applications for us to update. He will have them next week. Thelma Golightly, of SB County, came for her Monitor Review. She said we are ready. Recommendations given to contact one-stop manager for clients. Parents of two students came in to request that their daughters have Friday p.m. off due to their religion – Seventh Day Adventist. We will accommodate them. The father was so thankful he asked what he could do. I replied, "Pray for me," and he did. His words were answers to my prayer. He asked for protection and financial blessings to the school and me. I was grateful for his words.

Each day is God's gift. I appreciate it.

Thank You, Lord.

10/22/00 ~ 11:24 p.m.

I think this is the right date. Friday, Ernell, Jean Stevenson, her husband, Hershel, and I flew to Las Vegas. Jean and I went to the ABHES Conference. The men went to hang out with us. My focus was to research Las Vegas. It is a potential new training site. As I talked with individuals, Ernell at my side, I was sensing a severe lack of training for VN, but also a lack of encouragement from some. The executive director of the Urban Chamber was not hopeful, yet Brenda and Joanne were great. We toured the city, took numbers for Joanne to follow up on. I have much to do, research to follow up. I must stay focused and pray.

I attended the IEP Workshop and spoke briefly with Karen – a lady who did a monetary visit. She remembered me and my faith. It was good to hear her reflect on her remembrance of me and knowing God will keep us.

Back to the school, back to work. Lord, thank You.

241

10/27/00 ~ 11:58 p.m.

Another blessed day. Feeling a little anxious, a little upset, a little used. Zachary had called and left a message that he had an appearance in court. I knew he wanted me there so I cancelled my morning meeting. I arrived at County Superior Court at 8:35 a.m. I waited from 8:30 till 11:00 a.m. before I had the opportunity to speak with Zachary's attorney, Mr. Cantrell. He informed me that Zach had 3 strikes, but he was negotiating to have the last strike reduced to a misdemeanor. This change would reduce a possible '25 to life' down to 4 years. At 11:45 the judge called a break, but Zach's attorney had struck a deal with the prosecutor. He would have two strikes and receive credit of 20 months towards his sentences. He would receive four years. Zach could be out in 18 months. I thanked his attorney. I thank God. As I left the courthouse, I called Momma and shared the blessed news. Her heart was glad. Momma thanked me for being there. She told me she was proud of me. I stayed for her. After saying goodbye, I shed a few tears. Tears of joy for Zach and tears of frustration for my brother's activities and the emotional hardship they had placed on Momma.

Dr. Jane Smith, President of NCNW, along with Ms. Carson, Neicy, and others came to the Academy for a tour. Priscilla did an excellent job. They all were very proud of what we had done.

I attended New Gethsemane Church, Dr. Watts Pastor. I had been invited to attend a 'Sermons in Song' by Sister Watts. What a blessing. As the play dealt with the rapture of God, a young man in front of me began to cry during the scene of the gang shootout and casket. At the end of the program, he accepted the Lord. I was so touched by his actions. He raised both arms high above his head. He shouted, "I love Jesus!" The Spirit told me to talk with him. He was working hard to make it. He had transportation. I gave him my name, school name, and telephone number. I told him I would train him if he wanted to change his life, only he could not wear baggy jeans falling off his bottom. He was so appreciative. He knew Aja. I told him to have Aja take care of him. I had been given the position by God to help another. I am pleased with my life. Joseph will become a different person in 8 months.

Lord, thank You for selecting me.

10/29/00 ~ 7:34 a.m.

The last entry of this book.

Yesterday, Saturday 28, 2000, was a blessed day. The Inland Empire National Council of Negro Women Section hosted the 21st Annual Bethune Recognition Program. The event was held at the Double Tree in Ontario. The room was well laid out for 300 guests. Dr. Jane Smith, President of the National Organization, was the guest speaker. Carolyn Tillman was the Community Honoree for her Educational and Community Services. Lois Carson was the mistress of ceremony. I had the privilege of introducing Ms. Carson and Ms. Tillman. Dr. Gloria Morrow did the Benediction and Invocation. The message of Dr. Smith was our history: where we had come from, where we are, and where we are going. I wish we had recorded it. Following a wonderful program, there was picture-taking. The presidents of the chapters had a private meeting with Dr. Smith in Riverside at Mission Inn. At the end of the meeting, we did the Sister Circle, each one reflected on their blessings. I shared my blessing of Zachary and Joseph. Many were touched by my words and thanked me for sharing.

Following the meeting came the dinner. Priscilla Brown, Ms. Carson, Neicy Scott, Dr. Jane Smith, and I enjoyed a wonderful dinner and laughter for 2 ½ hours. We talked and laughed a while. Dr. Smith is extremely personable, friendly, and touchable. We exchanged home and work numbers. She stated clearly, "I am going to keep in touch with you." This morning, I told Ernell I expect I will make it onto the guest list for the National Office. I look forward to the networking growth, travel, and blessings for Four-D Success Academy from God.

Thank You, Lord.

11/5/00 ~ 8:25 p.m.

A new book begins. I had not purchased another journal as I had planned. So, here I am making my late entries. This past week has been filled with writing and meeting. The financial statement will be completed by Shawn on Nov. 30th. He placed a call to Christopher at ABHES, followed by a letter. I was concerned that the delay would create a problem for me, but I have been working on the financial audit report. Our review detected about a $30,000 error by the auditor. Tomorrow, I will mail my report certified to the US Department of Education. I need all of the delays I can get. I know it will work out for the good of the Academy. Last week, I met with Suzanna, ETP in San Diego. I am seeking another ETP contract. I was thinking along the line of 80. She was thinking 160; that's $672,000. I worked on the ETP contract this weekend. I completed my part. Now all I need is Betty and it will be off to San Diego Monday P.M.

Wendy and I have been doing the write-up for the SBA Business Person of the Year Award for me. As I have written the information, I have had memories of the beginning. I have done so much that I have forgotten to stop and reflect on the many wonderful things of the past. If I am selected, it will be a great testimony to Christ Jesus. All I am is because of Him. Each day, God blesses me with enough to fill the day. Last week, payroll was met, some bills paid without us going to the line of credit. For this, I am grateful.

I am seeking God's guidance on how to expand. I want to start a Medical Billing Service. Mona Houston told me to THINK BIG. The name will be ENCOMPASS: To include comprehensively. The services of Medical Billing and Health Clinics Examiners.

I must follow up with Las Vegas this coming week. I know that there is something for us. I pray to stay focused on the objective. God has blessed us another day. The doors remain open. For that, I am grateful.

Lord, guide my path. I pray to see where you want me to go. I follow not in fear, but in confidence.

Thank You, Lord.

11/7/00 ~ 8:00 a.m.

Yesterday, I spoke with Stephanie Evans. She was referred by Mona Houston. She and I discussed Medical Billing Services. I am going to open a Billing Service within the next 3 months. I know I will be successful in obtaining clients. I have work to do regarding cost of set up, computer, software, and marketing. But I know it will benefit the school and students. My goal is to create an externship for students through Encompass Billing Services.

Friends of Four-D Success were blessed. We received an approved list of items from the County of San Bernardino. Thursday, Mike,

Brian, and I will pick them up. God is good. I now prepare for a new day. Oh yes, the ETP Contract was completed and mailed. We made the deadline. The appeal was submitted to the U.S. Department of Education. The ETP Contract is for $672,000. I pray for approval and I pray we make it. I pray for clients who want to work and stay employed. I pray that the Appeal Board reduces our debt by $50,000+. The nomination for Business Person of the Year was submitted by Wendy/Eugene Gonzales. I am honored.

Lord, thank You.

11/13/00 ~ 7:45 a.m.

It seems as though it has been weeks since I have written in the diary. This past week, I spoke with Delores Weld, RN, MHA, from San Diego. She will consider developing the fast-track RN Program. I received a disc from Stephanie Evans for the development of a Medical Billing Service. ABHES Commissions met last Friday. I received a call regarding our default rate. The report of 100% was incorrect. As I process through the passages of time, I reflect on the multi-facet complexities I have had to cross. I pray for the time of total financial, student, and staff stability. I long for a month of absolute peace. I take the challenge. That's what makes this all work, but one month of rested nerves would be welcome.

Today, I must focus on Nevada, Bureau Renewal, and the audit. The best thing I know is that my Jesus, my Lord, is with me. As I continue to strive to give my best to Four-D Success Academy, the students, the staff, I know God gives His best to me. There has been much in the past and there will be much in the future.

I called Dr. Jane Smith yesterday. I wanted to thank her for her presentation at the Bethune Recognition Luncheon, and I thanked her for a great time at dinner. I was given permission to call her Jane. I look forward to a positive relationship. She is proud of the things I have done. My message of 'Take It Back' struck her with such force that she mentioned to me. "Take back what the Lord has given you." I pray for her continued success. Lord, bless us all as we do Your will.

Your Child, Linda

11/21/00 ~ 7:18 a.m.

The song 'I know the Lord will Make a Way' was in my voice as I woke up. My spirit was singing to the Lord. I know the Lord will make a way. Yes, He will. Dear Jesus, thank You for all You have given me. Thank You for my family, friends, and for Four-D Success Academy. Thank You for the prayers I am able to have with the students. Thank You for my joy and my peace. Thank You for Your personal love for me.

Last week, the Nursing Board approved our next class of 45 to enroll in January. Lord, I pray for a full class of students who are truly seeking the education and the foundation we have. I seek students for all of our programs. Fill our house, Lord. Yes, He will. We are preparing to submit our application to the Bureau for continued operations. I will submit a new program, the Medical Assistant Program with it. The Dental Program will be ready during the 1st quarter of 2001. The Child Care Program will be submitted in December. I know the Lord will make a way. Last evening, Dr. Fisher came to the school for a visit. He is quite impressed with our achievements. He extended his offer to help us in any way he can. I am awaiting the ABHES report. I know the Lord will make a way. Yes, He will.

Thank You, Jesus.

Linda L. Smith

11/26/00 ~ 9:37 p.m.

I awakened today with the desire to listen to sermons on T.V. There are times that I feel the Word for me is before me in my private room. Charles Stanley was teaching on the blessings of God, the faith that is needed to persevere, the focus that is needed to pursue the goals God has set for me, accepting the fact that God selected me to do His will. A bishop spoke on God's ability to place us above our enemy, above those who do not believe in God's plan for me (us), and of God's protection.

At some point, I began to cry as feelings rose up within me. I could feel God's presence. I cried. I thanked God for what I had. I prayed for Four-D Success Academy, the students, faculty, the school's finances, my family, and my husband.

Later in the early morning, Ernell brought me, to my surprise, breakfast in bed. I immediately began to cry, overwhelmed by his kindness and display of love.

I kneeled and prayed. I am thankful. For all that my life has encompassed, I am thankful.

My day was blessed. My time home, Thursday, Friday, Saturday, and Sunday has been a true blessing. I stayed inside all day Friday and Sunday. I loved every minute of it. My home, my life with my husband, and God. Peace is within me. Love abounds.

Lord, thank You.

Your Child, Linda

I appreciate all that you have given me. Thank You.

11/30/00 ~ 11:13 p.m.

The last couple of days have been interesting. Through the trials of the past, I've turned to trust in Jesus. Things will work out for good. The process to obtain our Business License has troubled me since September. OL Lacey and Company did not meet the requirements of the Fire Marshall. The sprinkler head had been moved prior to the plans being submitted or approved. The sprinkler service was required to draw a plan for approval. I have spent hours calling for follow-through. Finally, my spirit told me to let loose. It would work out. Today, a message came that the Fire Marshall and sprinkler service would be doing a walk through on Monday at 10:30 a.m. Although I don't know the outcome, it is a step in the right direction.

We will meet the deadline for December 31, 2000, to review our current license. ABHES granted us a 3-year accreditation – December 31, 2003. Lord, I am so very thankful. It took a year to obtain the renewal. I am thankful for the support of the ABHES staff and the supporting staff at Four-D Success Academy. Next, we will get the Bureau report off by December 8, 2000.

At 12:50 a.m., I will be on a flight to Wolfe City Texas to visit a great aunt, Tadie Johnson. She and I have never met. She is the youngest sibling of my great-grandmother M.W. Godspeed. I look forward to the visit. While there, I will visit two families I have been referred to by Charlie Seymour and Mike Williams.

Ernell is going to Mammoth to ski and Aisha will be taking the CBEST Test. God will protect us all and bring us back together as a family. We travel in His grace and protection. Lord, thank You for this day.

12/10/00 ~ 12:26 a.m.

I still have not purchased a new diary. So here are the latest entries.

On Thursday of last week, December 5th, I was in Texas. I flew to Wolfe City to visit Auntie Tadie Johnson. She is my great-grandmother's (M W Godspeed) baby sister. At the young age of 90, she is the last sibling alive. I had never met her, but I had heard about her through the years. Momma and Daddy had visited her on their travels to Texas. Auntie Tadie lives on a farm with her dog, Monica. The 49 acres, 16 cows, ponds, and trees were beautiful. I could not imagine the size. She and her husband purchased the property 35 years ago. He died in 1985 (15 years ago) at the age of 75. She was left to manage the farm. Well, she is fit to do so. She hauled in wood a dozen times a day and refused my help. She drives a car and truck and she is thinking of buying an SUV. An exercise bike is in her bedroom. She stated she used to exercise regularly but she developed a hernia. But since it had healed, she would resume at some point. Exercise made her feel alive and energetic. My visit was to meet this wonderful lady. I had only heard of my auntie, my great-grandmother's baby sister. I visited, rested. We rose at 11:30-12:00 noon on Saturday/Sunday. I was truly exhausted, but we stayed up until midnight. On Saturday, we were up until 3:00 a.m. after receiving a short visit from James, Andrew, and Laura. I knew it would not be easy to leave on Wednesday December 5th. How do you say goodbye? I rose, packed my bags, and ate breakfast. Hearing sadness in her voice saddened me. I will return soon.

ABHES gave us an approval until December 2003. For this, I am grateful. The financial audit still must be submitted. I pray to God we are not placed on a review once it is submitted.

The Bureau Report will be submitted next week. It is due on February 28, 2001, allowing ample time for review.

South Bay PIC (Private Industry Council) finally came out to review the Beaumont site. I expect approval.

As I address issues at the school, I try to provide the necessary guidance, which will enhance our performance. Michael Williams was promoted to the position of Director of Developmental Operations and Strategic Planning. I expect some significant changes in admissions, enrollment, and marketing. He is excited and I knew he would do well.

Jean Stevenson is the Employee of the Year. The LVN Program was rewritten, the pass rate increased from 17% to 71%.

Ann Logan will receive the Exceptional Service Certificate for her role in the Financial Aid Department.

Lord, we are coming up to the end of 2000. You have brought us this far. Against all odds, Your grace and mercy have seen us through. We are so thankful. I pray that You will bless us abundantly. Show me the direction to go. Prepare us to take on a hundred-fold clients. Grow us to the best. Keep our spirit alive. Keep our focus on You. Guide our path. We thank You for the past year of trial and tribulations for they have made us stronger in Your presence and in our trust and faith in You.

Thank You so very much.

12/18/00 ~ 10:41 p.m.

I still have not purchased a new journal. So I must continue to make entries on notepaper. My trip to Texas was more enjoyable and

Linda L. Smith

relaxing than I realized. I am still sharing my trip to others. I must return next year.

The presentation to the ETP Board was painless. I flew to San Francisco on the 13th, made a presentation on the 14th, and received approval to train 160 clients for $630,000. Betty and I must strategize how to best market, recruit, and retain the clients.

The Bureau report is ready for submission tomorrow. This morning, Danetra called at 6:00 a.m. to tell me her brother passed. She would start the Dental Assistant Program in January. I gave my condolences for her loss. This is truly a season of loss. This is the 3rd person I know who has lost a loved one in the last 30 days. Charlie Seymour has not recovered. Today, he was admitted to Board via Christian Science Facility. He sounded fine this p.m. He is happy to be there. So am I. He was losing weight, not eating, low energy, etc. This environment will aid his recovery. I know he will be okay.

Delores Weld called today. She confirmed she will develop the RN Program for us. I am so excited about this. We will have the Medical Assistant Program, Dental Program, RN Program, Child Care Program, and the Encompass Billing Service. This will truly be a fulfilled 2000. I must stay prayed up and focused.

Lord, guide me.

Thank You.

Linda

Looking Back ...

- Getting to the Promised Land is an adventure! Through many hills and valleys, I trust Him to see me through. Fair-weather friends may forsake me, business acquaintances may look the other way, but the glory of the Lord is constant in and out of season.

- This has been a journey unlike any other.

- I can never be afraid of the numbers. When God's hands are involved, situations and dollars become bigger.

- We generate that which we are. When I am calm and peaceful, the atmosphere reciprocates that energy. When I am full of faith, I see the results of my faith. I have, however, had moments when I have behaved less than a child of God should. It is during those times that my humanness reflects, and I am reminded that I am to lean on Him every single day no matter what — good and bad times requires me to trust in Him all the more because the situation is subject to change!

- The messengers of the Lord will come from a horizon of places; be sure to keep an ear to the throne. Just like dreams, prophecies come true too!

- Maintaining healthy relationships is crucial when you purpose to stay focused. Guard your inner circle with all your heart because they will be the ones you draw strength from. These same people will keep you lifted up when things become daunting, and they will celebrate your successes without envy.

253

- One man's trash, another man's treasure! Never be too proud to accept material donations. An open attitude allows the Lord to send you just what you need, right when you need it most. Second hand doesn't mean second best — it simply comes with experience!

- Stand, stand, and remain standing when you have done all that you know to do, and watch the Lord work it out in your favor if you would only believe.

- Going from two students to thousands has not been without heartache; yet the rewards continue to be far greater than I ever imagined. Little really does become much when you place it in the Master's hands.

- Trust is not an option; it's a necessity. He won't let you be ashamed when you put all your energy into what you believe He has commissioned you to do. Trust Him to see you through.

- Expansion comes through relationship with the Lord. You want Him to enlarge your territory? Get to know Him.

Success will follow as you pursue the plans you have been given. Events will shape your journey. People will add value to your purpose even when they allow themselves to be used and work *against* your efforts.

I have been very fortunate to make a living doing what I love and am passionate about. Four-D College is the vehicle in which God extends Himself through me to assist others. And just as exciting are the many, many wonderful people that God has allowed me to work with. Together, we inspire and challenge women and men to press beyond their immediate circumstances, and reach toward a lifestyle they can be proud of by educating themselves, a life that allows them to become pillars of society, and instruments of hope.

We all make a choice day after day to impart wisdom, inspiration, and love to our fellowman. Without much thought, we can choose to be divisive, negative, visionless, unproductive, and a menace to society. It is my prayer that after reading the three volumes of *Business by Faith*, that you have been inspired to serve others in whatever capacity you choose to. Just be certain that it's a road well lit by the light of love from above. In time, your legacy will speak for itself.

About the Author

Linda L. Smith, a Registered Nurse for 35 years, combined her love of Nursing, high standards of health care professionalism, and deep spiritual faith, and founded the first and only African-American owned, fully accredited vocational career college in California licensed to teach Vocational Nursing and other allied health care programs. The institution has been recognized as an Outstanding Business by numerous agencies.

Linda has been featured in *Essence Magazine,* is a contributor to the book *Creating Value through People,* and authored *Business by Faith, Integrating the 4D's of Success Personally and Professionally.* In October 2013 a documentary, *Linda L. Smith, A Profile In Courage,* was released and received the Accolade Award.

She was appointed Vice President Board of Trustees for the Inland Empire Loma Linda Ronald McDonald House and to the California State Assistance Fund for Enterprise, Business and Industrial Development Corporation Board of Directors by Governor Brown's Office.

As Founder of Four-D College and an inspirational speaker, she helps women and men pursue their vision with confidence.

Speaking at Colleges, Universities, Conferences, and other events designed to support those pursuing success, particularly in the Health Care Industry and Entrepreneurship/Business and Leadership, Linda teachers her 4D's of Success Personally and Professionally, imparting valuable information to help those who desire to start up a business, or progress in their current business or career path. She shows them how to overcome challenges and achieve success in business and in life.

Her experiences are soul-stirring, her message is powerful, and her delivery is profound. The way in which she shares her personal story, including struggles and adversity, is both educational and empowering.

To book Linda to speak at your event, contact her at www.lindalsmith.com or linda@lindalsmith.com.

www.ingramcontent.com/pod-product-compliance
Lightning Source LLC
Chambersburg PA
CBHW071627200326
41519CB00012BA/2194